# PETER AND HIS LORD

## Sermons on the Life of Peter

By

### CLARENCE EDWARD MACARTNEY

MINISTER, FIRST PRESBYTERIAN CHURCH, PITTSBURGH, PA.

ABINGDON PRESS

NEW YORK   •   NASHVILLE

PETER AND HIS LORD

*Copyright MCMXXXVII by Whitmore & Smith*

I

SET UP, PRINTED, AND BOUND BY THE
PARTHENON PRESS, AT NASHVILLE,
TENNESSEE, UNITED STATES OF AMERICA

# FOREWORD

Not until one makes a careful study of the life of Peter does one realize what a prominent place he takes in the Gospels and in the Book of Acts. Leave him out, and many of the most instructive, moving, and dramatic passages of the New Testament are gone.

The ground for these sermons was first broken in a series of addresses at the Wednesday Night Service. Some years afterwards these preliminary sketches were developed into a series of sermons preached at the Sunday morning services.

With a few exceptions, all the major events of Peter's life are taken up in these sermons. Biographical preaching always makes its appeal; especially when the preacher has for his hero a character like Peter.

[5]

# CONTENTS

# PETER'S CALL

## I

### *"And he brought him to Jesus"*
John 1: 42

### *"Fear not; from henceforth thou shalt catch men"*
Luke 5: 10

" AND Peter!" That was what the Young Man said to the women at the sepulcher. "Tell his disciples, and Peter." There was a special message for Peter, just as there was a special Resurrection appearance to Peter.

Peter always stands out. When you have spoken of the Twelve Apostles, you must speak in a special manner of Peter. After you have sketched the Apostles, there is always a particular additional word to be spoken about Peter.

Peter is the most vivid and intense personality portrayed in the Bible. There is none like him. In any group of the Apostles it is always easy to pick out Peter. The reason for this is that Peter's portrait is painted by two great artists. One was Christ himself—what he said to Peter. To no other disciple did Christ speak so frequently. To no other disciple did he utter such promises, predictions, rebukes, warnings, prayers, encouragement, blessing, and high commission. That alone would set Peter off by himself.

The other great artist who sketches Peter is Peter himself. Matthew, Mark, Luke, and John tell the story of Peter; but we must remember that it is Peter himself who is talking through these men. First of all, there are the words of Peter, what Peter said to Jesus; his memorable confessions, his rash remonstrances, his prayer when he was sinking in the sea, his question about the limit of forgiveness, his protest that Christ should not wash his feet; his boastful affirmation of loyalty, his oaths of denial, his tears when Christ looked upon him, and that final and beautiful word, "Thou knowest that I love thee!"

Then there are the *acts* of Peter. If the Gospels recorded nothing that Peter said, still we would know him better than any of the other disciples because of the way he acts, sometimes nobly, sometimes basely; but always impulsively. His falling down at the feet of Christ in the fishing boat, his attempt to walk on the sea, his cutting off the ear of the servant of the high priest, his race with John to the tomb, his leap into the sea when he saw Jesus on the shore—what a world is Peter! What faith, doubt, weakness, strength, courage, cowardice, what impetuous love! Take Peter out of the Gospels, and the story has lost much of its color and its interest. Leave Peter in, and let all the rest go, and still in what Christ said to Peter, and in what Peter said to Christ, and in what Peter did, you have a Gospel that can be preached to the ends of the earth, wherever a human heart beats.

Peter was called twice, first as a disciple and then as an Apostle. He is always first in the catalogue of the Apostles; but he was not the first of the disciples.

John the Baptist was baptizing beyond Jordan. Andrew and Simon and John, and, no doubt, James, although he is not mentioned, had left their nets and their fishing to go out to listen to John. He was the great religious voice and leader of the day. He represented the best and the highest; and, therefore, they went out to hear him and to follow him beyond the Jordan. Andrew and John, we know, became disciples first of the Baptist. It is altogether likely, too, that Peter was a disciple of John, and had been baptized in the Jordan.

On the second day after the baptism of Jesus by John, Andrew and the other John were in the company of the Baptist when Jesus passed by. How much that is great in the history of mankind seems to hinge upon chance meetings. Suppose that Jesus had not passed by at that time! Suppose that Andrew and John had not heard what the Baptist had said of Jesus! What they heard him say was this,

and it was Christianity in all its length and breadth
and depth and height: "Behold the Lamb of God, that
taketh away the sin of the world."

That was what attracted Andrew and John to
Jesus. That was why they followed him and said to
him, "Master, where dwellest thou?" Andrew and
John knew what the Lamb of God meant, that it stood
for the forgiveness of sins through the great Act
of One who was to come. That always is the attrac-
tion and the magnet of the Cross, the Lamb of God
slain from the foundation of the world. All else is
secondary and subordinate. Like Paul after him,
John the Baptist declared unto men, "first of all,"
that Christ died for our sins, according to the Scriptures. John's declaration was the first Christian
sermon. It will be the last Christian sermon, when
the great multitude and every creature in heaven
and on earth shall ascribe majesty and dominion and
glory unto him that sitteth upon the throne, and
to the Lamb forever and ever.

What was said at that memorable interview between Jesus and Andrew and John we know not, but
we do know the great result. They came away convinced that Jesus was the Christ, the Messiah, the
One for whom the ages had waited. It was a memorable hour for John and Andrew. John had other
great hours in his experience as a Christian. He
stood with Jesus on the Mount of Transfiguration,
leaned on his breast at the Supper, saw him die on the

Cross, saw him ascend into heaven, and on Patmos saw him standing in the midst of the Seven Golden Candlesticks with the Seven Stars in his Right Hand. But this was the great hour for John. Writing perhaps half a century or more afterwards, he remembers the exact time of the day, how high the sun was in heaven, and tells us in his Gospel, "It was about the Tenth Hour."

The first thing that Andrew did when he had come to know that Jesus was the Messiah was to find Peter and bring him to Jesus, saying, "We have found the Christ." When Jesus looked upon Peter and saw his great possibilities, he uttered these prophetic words: "Thou art Simon: thou shalt be called Cephas, which is by interpretation, a stone." Christ knew what was in Peter; all his weakness, but also that here was the material for a great life, for a rock upon which men could build.

— The second call of Peter was to the Apostleship. It was morning by the Sea of Galilee. To be free from the press of the crowd that followed him, Jesus borrowed Peter's fishing boat and used it as a pulpit from which he preached to the crowd on the shore. He might have borrowed Andrew's boat, or John's, or James', or some other's, but it was Peter's boat that he borrowed. Peter loaned Jesus his boat and his house; another loaned him the foal of an ass; another the Upper Chamber; another, a soldier, loaned him his sponge at the Cross; Simon the Cyrenian

loaned him his shoulder with which to carry the
Cross; Joseph of Arimathea loaned him his grave;
and the women loaned him their spices. There is always something—time, money, strength, sacrifice,
prayer, hope—that we can loan to Christ. When we
see him in the Day of Judgment, may each one of us
be able to recognize him as the One to whom we
loaned something.

When the sermon was over, Jesus said to Peter,
"Launch out into the deep, and let down your nets
for a draught." Peter's face was always a mirror
and never a masque, and you can almost see the look
of amazement and half amusement in Peter's countenance when he heard what Jesus said. "Fish at this
time of the forenoon when the hot sun is on the sea?
Master, this is not the time we catch fish. It's at
night and in the early morning. You understand
the work of the carpenter, but you are not familiar
with fishing." Then Peter adds, "Nevertheless at thy
word I will let down the net." That is all the church
has, the Christian minister, the Christian worker as
the authority, and for the hope, of our labors—the
Word of Jesus. You can see Peter's brawny arms
as with impulsive, impatient strokes he helps to pull
the boat out into the middle of the lake. Every
movement and look of Peter is as much as to say,
"It's no use; but since he asks it we will do it." But
when they had let down the nets and the fish were
running into them so that the boat was like to sink,

then Peter in amazement halloos for his partners, Andrew, and James, and John, to come and help him land the fish. When the haul is brought on board, then what did Peter do? What did he say? Did he say, "Lord, you *are* a fisherman after all! How did you learn it? We will make you a partner in our business. Henceforth it is Andrew, Peter, James and John, sons of Zebedee, *and* Jesus"? No; that is not what Peter said. He fell at the feet of Jesus amid the nets and the fishes and cried out, "Depart from me; for I am a sinful man, O Lord."

Here is an instance of how Christ made use of Peter, one of the least thoughtful and reflective of the Apostles, to teach sublime truths about himself and the way of salvation. In the presence of Christ Peter saw himself to be a sinner. That is the first fact of a real Christian experience. What Christ means to us depends upon our sense of need as a sinner. Only when we are conscious of our sin can we lay hold on Christ as he is offered to us in the Scriptures and in the Gospels. It is not the Sermon on the Mount which shows us our deepest need of Christ and brings home most our sinfulness, but the Eternal Sermon which was preached on the Cross, when the Lamb of God suffered and died for our sins.

Peter cried out, "Depart from me, O Lord, for I am a sinful man!" But Christ said to him, "Fear not; from henceforth thou shalt catch men." Peter has learned the first great lesson of the Christian life;

now he will soon be ready to let down his net into the deep sea of humanity and catch men.

That was Peter's call as an Apostle. But his first call was as a disciple, and that call came to him through his brother Andrew. If you look at the history of the great men, you will see standing back of them, or at one side, and somewhat in the shadow, another man. It is the figure of one who helped them, counseled them, predicted great things for them, and encouraged them. Andrew brought Peter to Christ, and then disappears from the scene. We hardly hear of him again. But he had done his great work. Barnabas vouched for Saul of Tarsus when everybody at Jerusalem and elsewhere looked upon him with suspicion; and when, years later, the work of the Spirit began among the Greek-speaking Gentiles at Antioch, it was Barnabas who went up to Tarsus and brought Paul down to Antioch and thus set him upon the arena of his great work. Henceforth, it is all Paul in the Book of the Acts. Barnabas soon disappears altogether. But he had done his work.

Who today, unless he reads in that field, remembers the name of the monk who at Erfurt took the time and the pains to instruct the young Luther at the crisis of his life and taught him to cast his reliance upon Christ crucified for his salvation? Who remembers the name of the lay preacher who on a stormy January Sabbath in 1850 mounted the pulpit of the Primitive Methodist Chapel in Artillery

Street and gave out the text, "Look unto me and be ye saved, all the ends of the earth"? But everyone knows today the name of the boy who was sitting in the back seat of the gloomy church and, in answer to that text, looked and was saved and was gloriously used of God to save others. It was Charles Spurgeon. Who recalls the name of that Sunday school teacher in the Mount Vernon Congregational Church, Boston, who, with the burden of one of his boys on his heart, walked up and down several times in front of the shoe store where that boy was employed, and then, finally mustering up his courage, walked to the back of the store where he found the boy wrapping up shoes, and laying his hand on his shoulder, said some faltering words about how Christ loved him. But this year the whole Christian world will celebrate the centennial of the birth of that boy, for he was Dwight L. Moody. Moody could never forget the thrill of that moment, and how he felt after Kimball had spoken to him. "I went out of doors and I fell in love with the bright sun shining over the earth. I never loved the sun before, and when I heard the birds singing their sweet song on Boston Common, I fell in love with the birds. I was in love with all creation."

Peter's greatest monument is the noble church at Rome which bears his name. Standing under the vast dome one can read there the words of our Lord to Peter, "Thou art Peter, and upon this rock I will build my Church; and the gates of hell shall not prevail against it." But sometimes when I stand in St. Peter's and look up to the dome and read those words of Christ to Peter, I see another name and another inscription. It is this: "Thou art Andrew, the man who brought Peter to Christ."

The Church does not need more theology, more philanthropy, more organization. What it needs is more Andrews. The Church does not need another Paul. You cannot reproduce him. One Paul does forever. The Church does not need another John. There was but one John. The Church does not need another Peter. God made but one and then broke the die. But the Church does need another Andrew, the man who brings other men to Christ. Peter and John and Paul are beyond us all. We can never do their work. But we can do, if we will, the work of Andrew, the man who brought Peter to Christ.

# PETER'S CONFESSION

## II

### *"Thou art the Christ, the Son of the living God"*

Matthew 16: 16

IN a letter written to the Roman Emperor Trajan by Pliny the Younger, Governor of Bithynia, a province along the Black Sea, about the year 110 A.D., Pliny describes what he has learned about the Christians and their worship. "They are accustomed to meet," he says, "on a fixed day before daylight to sing a hymn of praise to Christ as God."

The troubled governor of Bithynia, trying to give an explanation to the Roman emperor of the spread of the Christian faith, so rapid that it was leaving the pagan altars deserted, unwittingly declared the secret of the power of Christianity and its spread in the world.

The Christians worshiped Jesus Christ as God. That Christ is God, is the heart and the power of Christianity. All Christian history, creeds, councils, theologies, Scriptures, past conquests, and future victories are summed up in that sentence, "They worshiped Christ as God." It fell to the Apostle Peter to make the most memorable declaration of that Faith, that Jesus Christ is God.

Peter's confession of Christ as the Messiah and the Son of God came at a crisis in his ministry. The popular favor had declined from him and he was no longer a national hero. Opposition and persecution had made it wise for him to withdraw from the populous districts in which he had been working, and he retired to the region of Caesarea Philippi, a district near Mount Hermon, far to the north. One has described the site of this Caesarea in these words: "The fertile plains of Huleh surround it. The goodly mountain Hermon overshadows it. The sparkling rivulets from the sources of the Jordan water it. Thickets of oleanders, groves of oaks and olives, clusters of hawthorn and myrtle adorn it, and the grand old castle of Subeibeh, standing solitary on the hilltop, watches over it like a gardener." On the slope of Hermon is a cliff with ancient inscriptions, and niches where the statues of the gods once stood. In a cavern at the foot of the cliff the worship of the shepherd god Pan was celebrated, and from this cavern flows the spring which is the source of the river Jordan. It is quite possible that our Lord on this visit saw this pagan shrine and the statues of the gods. This, then, was the scene of the declaration of the first great Christian creed, the beginning of that grand stream of Christian confession of faith which has flowed down through the ages.

Jesus said to his disciples, "Whom do men say that I the Son of man am?" This was an extraordinary question. They all knew who he was and where he came from, in the ordinary sense of the word. Yet Jesus said, "Whom do men say that I am?" No other teacher or prophet could have asked such a question. We cannot imagine Moses, or Elijah, or Isaiah, or St. Paul, or St. Peter, asking of men, "Who am I?" These great teachers and prophets raised no question as to their personality or nature. Everyone knew, no matter what their powers or their office, or how gifted, that they were men of like passions with the rest of humanity. But, inevitably, Christ raises this question, "Who art thou?" You say you will follow his example, and seek to do his will, and obey his words, regardless of who he is, whether he be the Eternal Son of God or just the best, or one of the best and greatest of mankind. But unless he is the Son of God, unless he speaks and acts with the power of God, how do you know that his example is the best, that his precepts are the wisest, that his words have authority?

When Benjamin Franklin, toward the end of his life, was asked by his friend, Ezra Stiles, President of Yale College, to declare himself on this subject of the Person of Christ, Franklin answered that he considered his system of morals and religion the

best the world ever saw or is like to see, but that he
has some doubts as to his Divinity. He will not
trouble himself much about the subject now, because
so soon he will have "an opportunity of knowing the
truth with less trouble." Then he goes on to say
that probably belief in the divinity of Christ makes
his doctrines more respected and more observed.
There is no question as to that. That, indeed, is
true, and far more than that. There are those who
do not subscribe to the deity of our Lord, and who
could not confess with Peter, "Thou art the Son of
the living God." Yet they revere his Person, study
his words, and endeavor to follow his example. But
the important thing to remember is, that unless in
the beginning, and through the ages, there had been
those who stood where Peter stood and confessed
what Peter confessed, we would never have heard of
the example, or the teachings, or the beautiful spirit,
or even the Person of Christ. All that we know and
love about Christ, we owe to those who confessed and
followed him as the Son of God.

The disciples told Jesus the opinions that were
current concerning him. Some took him to be John
the Baptist. John the Baptist had already been put
to death by Herod Antipas. The people, some of
them, surmised that the spirit of mighty John had
reappeared in the Person of Jesus. This was the
opinion of Herod himself, for when the works of
Jesus were attracting wide attention, Herod dis-

missed all other explanations and identifications, and said, "It is John whom I beheaded. He is risen from the dead." The guilty conscience of Herod, who had murdered John to please his wife, affirmed that Jesus was John come back to life.

Others thought that he was Elijah, because of the prediction in the last book of the Old Testament, Malachi: "Behold, I will send you Elijah the prophet before the great and terrible day of the Lord come." Elijah played a great part in the imagination and expectation of the people. Many had been sure that John the Baptist was Elijah, and now that John had disclaimed such a character, and was himself dead and buried, they transferred the identification to Jesus. Jesus must be the great Elijah.

Still others thought that he was Jeremiah. Jeremiah was one of the great figures, not only in the history, but in the expectation of the Hebrew people. There was a tradition current, that he had appeared to the Hebrew hero Judas Maccabaeus, and had given him a golden sword, the gift of God, with which to wage war for the deliverance of the Chosen People. Still others, while not venturing to say which one of the prophets, were sure that a great prophet had risen again in Christ. These were not the only opinions. The Scribes and Pharisees regarded him as an impostor: "That deceiver," as they said to Pilate when they requested a guard at his tomb. There were others who regarded him as beside himself; and still others thought that he was possessed of the devil, and that that accounted for his mighty works. But Jesus dismissed the popular opinions about himself, and said with great emphasis to the disciples, "But whom say ye that I am?" Then it was that Peter broke forth with his grand confession, "Thou art the Christ, the Son of the living God."

In a sense, there was nothing new about this conviction that Jesus was the Christ. Andrew and John, after that memorable first day with Christ, came away with the conviction that Jesus was the Christ, for Andrew went at once to find Peter and said to him, "We have found the Messiah." Philip must have believed the same thing when he brought Nathanael to Jesus, for he said, "We have found him, of whom Moses in the law, and the prophets, did write." The demons who had been cast out of the man in the synagogue at Capernaum cried out that Jesus was the Holy One of God; and on the night that Christ walked on the sea, and saved Peter from drowning when he attempted to do likewise, the disciples, filled with awe, exclaimed, "Of a truth, thou art the Son of God."

But there was a deliberation, an enthusiasm, a conviction and exultation in the confession of Peter that made this declaration differ from everything that had gone before. Whatever ideas had been entertained in the past as to the person of the Messiah, whether just a mighty human personality, or a divine personality, here Peter, and the other apostles with him, declare that Christ is the Son of the living God. This truth is the Alpha and Omega, the Beginning and the End, of the Christian faith. Here in the presence of Jesus himself, from the mouth of Peter, and in the midst of the Twelve Disciples, goes up the music of the first Christian creed, the first Confession of Faith, a music which sounds grandly from age to age, and will reach its grand climax when the ten thousand times ten thousand, and thousands of thousands shall say, "Worthy is the Lamb that was slain to receive power, and riches, and wisdom, and strength, and honor, and glory, and blessing."

There is an old Latin formula, which expresses the truth about the Church and its creeds. It runs like this: A Church without a creed is nothing. Some today hold the idea which was once expressed by Channing, the eloquent New England Unitarian, that as long as we do the will of Christ, it makes little difference what opinions we hold about his Person. If Jesus Christ is only a man, then follow him, they say, for his teaching is the purest that ever fell from human lips, and his example is the noblest. If he is God, still you can do no more than to follow him and obey him. But beliefs such as this never founded the Church and never kept it in the world through the storms of the ages. Only a Jesus who is the Eternal Son of God can redeem man from his sin; only the Divine Christ can be the object of our hope and our worship. Peter's confession at Caesarea Philippi is the first note in the grand music of the *Te Deum*, "Thou art the Everlasting Son of the Father."

The greatness of what Peter had confessed is evident from what our Lord at once said to him: "Blessed art thou, Simon Bar-jona; for flesh and blood hath not revealed it unto thee, but my Father which is in heaven." As Christ has been revealed in the world as the Son of God, whoever believes upon him has, in a sense, a divine revelation. Faith is our greatest possession. It is God's greatest gift to man. It is the highest expression of man's soul. Peter had other great moments in his life: when he stood upon the Mount and saw Christ transfigured, when he defied the conspirators in the Garden with his sword, when the Pentecostal Power came down upon him and he preached at Jerusalem, and when the angel smote him on the side and delivered him out of Herod's prison. But this was Peter's greatest moment, when, inspired by the Holy Spirit, he saw and confessed and declared Jesus to be the Christ, the Son of the living God; and there, too, we see man at his highest and greatest, when he confesses Jesus as the Son of God and the Saviour of the world.

The next words of Jesus, "Thou art Peter, and upon this rock I will build my church," have occasioned endless dispute. But whatever differences of opinion there are, and have been, as to the meaning of the "rock," whether Christ meant Peter, or himself, or the truth to which Peter had confessed, his Divine Sonship, his Deity, the one thing about which all Christians and all Churches can agree is the next statement, "The gates of hell shall not prevail against it." Here hell, or, to be exact, Hades, "as the shadow world of the dead, the unseen counterpart of the visible grave, all-absorbing, all destructive, into whose jaws or gates all things human pass, and from which issue all forces that destroy, is personified as a power, or a kingdom of death." In the Apocalypse, Death rides forth upon a pale horse, and Hell follows after him, "and power was given unto them over the fourth part of the earth, to kill with sword, and with hunger, and with death, and with the beasts of the earth." When Christ, therefore, says that the gates of death shall not prevail against the Church he declares that all the confederate powers of evil and of darkness that are united against God and against his Christ shall not prevail. His Kingdom is an Everlasting Kingdom. "No weapon," says the spirit in Isaiah of Christ's Kingdom and His Church, "no weapon that is formed against thee shall prosper."

There is nothing in the history of the nineteen centuries which have elapsed since Christ spoke these words to make us think that they will not be fulfilled. Power after power, kingdom after kingdom, philosophy after philosophy, fashion after fashion, heresy after heresy, Antichrist after Antichrist, has risen against the Church of Christ and sought to destroy it. Yet the Church endures. When the angel spoke to Joseph, and the mother of Jesus in Egypt, telling them to return to Palestine, he said, "They that sought the young child's life are dead." When Herod was dead! Every chapter in the long conflict of the world with the Church comes to a conclusion with that sentence, "They that sought the young child's life are dead." Herods die, but Christ lives forever.

Clouds and darkness are round about us today. Satan's chain of liberty seems to be longer than ever before, his mask more impenetrable, and his malice, his rage, and his subtlety more powerful than ever before, and it would seem as if even the elect are deceived. But be of good courage! Christ has spoken; His Word shall not fail. "Upon this rock I will build my church, and the gates of hell shall not prevail against it."

> "O where are kings and empires now,
>   Of old that went and came?
> But, Lord, thy Church is praying yet,
>   A thousand years the same." [1]

Let us take these words, that question of Jesus, "Whom say ye that I am?" and apply them each one to himself. You know what the Bible thinks of Jesus, you know what Peter, and John, and Paul,

----

[1] From hymn by Bishop A. Cleveland Coxe.

what Augustine and Luther and Calvin, your father and mother, your minister, think of Jesus; but the important thing for you is, what do *you* believe concerning Jesus? Whom do you say that he is? This is an age which discounts belief; but the Bible does not discount belief. Neither does Christ nor the Apostles. This is what the Bible says about belief in Christ: "With the heart man believeth unto righteousness; and with the mouth confession is made unto salvation." "If thou shalt confess with thy mouth the Lord Jesus, and shalt believe in thine heart that God hath raised him from the dead, *thou shalt be saved.*"

# PETER WALKING ON THE SEA

## III

### *"Lord, if it be thou, bid me come unto thee on the water"*

Matthew 14: 28

SPEAKING one night in a rescue mission in Philadelphia, I noticed over the platform a great mural painting of this memorable scene on the Sea of Galilee. Peter is sinking in the waves, but Christ stretches out his hand to save him. An appropriate painting, I thought, for the walls of a rescue mission; and all the more interesting because it had been painted by a man who had been saved and brought to Christ in that very mission. Christ had stretched forth his hand and saved him from the depths of drunkenness and sin. The painting was the token of his gratitude.

After Jesus had fed the five thousand, the multitude, stirred by such a miracle, sought to take him by force and make him a King. With such a wonder-worker for a king and leader, they said among themselves, we could brush the Roman legions out of Syria and restore the kingdom unto Israel It was the same temptation with which the devil tried to turn him aside from his chosen path when he took him to the top of an exceeding high mountain, and in a moment of time showed him the glory and the splendor of this world. But once again Satan came and found nothing in Him. Jesus constrained his unwilling disciples to get into the ship and start across the lake toward Capernaum on the western shore, dismissed the cheering multitudes, and instead of heading a procession of revolutionists, went up into a mountain to pray. "And when the evening was come, he was there alone."

## The Mount of Prayer

Jesus was such a busy man, ever going about doing good, that he had to choose the night for his meditations. Sometimes he went into the desert. When the mountains were at hand, and in that land they always are, he climbed a mountain, as if to lift himself for a little above the sin and coarseness of fallen humanity. The Church has been careful through the ages to repeat the prayer which our Lord taught his disciples; but have we been as eager to follow his example and manner, not only in the words of prayer, but in the time and place of prayer?

We read of just one mountain of Transfiguration, but I doubt not that if we had seen his face on any of those frequent mountaintops of prayer, we would have wondered at its glory. The great Minister to human need and sorrow climbed the hills to replenish his strength and quench his thirst at the ever-flowing fountain of prayer. As he climbed the side of the mountain that night, higher and higher, until the fishing boat on the moonlit sea of Tiberias was just a black speck, perhaps he repeated to himself the Psalm of the mountains, "I will lift up mine eyes unto the hills, from whence cometh my help."

If Christ had need of these times of solitude and refreshment, we certainly do in our lives. The cause of frequent overthrow and spiritual depression is the neglect of the ministry of prayer. Instead of looking to the hills, to the highest, to God, for help and strength, men look to their occupations, their diversions, their friends. Ours is a generation which fears to be alone. We crave the fever and bustle of excitement, of the multitude. Our life in the valley and on the plains would be stronger and nobler did we observe the seasons when we confer not with flesh and blood, but climb the mountain and look at ourselves and others and life in the light of prayer. Consumption of the body is cured by breathing the pure air of the mountains. Consumption of the soul is arrested by breathing the atmosphere of prayer.

"Lord, what a change within us one short hour
Spent in Thy presence will avail to make!
What heavy burdens from our bosoms take!
What parched ground refresh as with a shower!

We kneel, and all around us seems to lower;
  We rise, and all, the distant and the near,
  Stand forth in sunny outline, brave and clear.
We kneel—how weak! we rise—how full of power!
  Why, therefore, should we do ourselves this wrong,
  Or others, that we are not always strong,
That we are sometimes overborne with care—
  That we should ever weak or heartless be,
Anxious or troubled, when with us is prayer,
  And joy and strength and courage are with Thee?" [1]

## CONTRARY WINDS

Jesus was on the mountain praying. But the disciples were struggling with the storm in the midst of the sea. The Sea of Galilee lies six hundred feet below the level of the Mediterranean, and the rivers which flow into the sea have cut deep gorges through which the wind rushes as through a funnel, in a moment lashing the lake into angry waves.

The sea of life, like the Sea of Galilee, has contrary winds. Duty is never easy. The disciples had not desired to make this voyage. Jesus had to *constrain* them to enter into the ship. It was, therefore, plainly his will that they should battle nine hours with angry and contrary winds. Because a man becomes a believer and a disciple of Christ, he has no right to expect that from now on the winds will always be favorable. God sent a contrary wind

[1] Archbishop R. C. Trench.

against Jonah, fleeing from the Word of the Lord; and he sent a contrary wind against the disciples, obeying the Word of the Lord. The contrary wind, the north wind of trial and temptation and adversity, must blow upon us as well as the south and the soft wind. That was what the maiden of the Song of Songs prayed for her garden: "Awake, O north wind; and come, thou south; blow upon my garden, that the spices thereof may flow out."

Steel is made in the furnace, and there is no wine until the grapes are crushed. In a day when his struggles and hardships were behind him, Charles Lamb wrote of those struggles and contrary winds against which he and his sister Mary had fought together: "That we had much to contend with as we grew up together, we have reason to be most thankful. It strengthened and knit our compact closer together. We never would have been what we have been to each other if we had always had the sufficiency which you now complain of." The strongest characters are those who have faced the contrary winds. "They that go down to the sea in ships, that do business in great waters; these see the works of the Lord, and his wonders in the deep."

## THE SYMPATHY OF CHRIST

Mark, in his always graphic narrative, tells us that Jesus saw them toiling in rowing. Up by his mountain altar he could see the lightning flash and the storm sweep down the lake, and the disciples toiling to bring the boat to the land. He was watching them. Never once did they get beyond the range of his eye. But the disciples did not know that he saw them. Perhaps they feared that he had forgotten all about them. I can imagine impulsive Peter as he toiled at the oar, or held the tiller, saying, "I wonder if the Master does not care that we perish?" Or melancholy Thomas saying, "What is the use of struggling with the oars any longer? The ship is going down! The Master has forgotten us!"

This is the story of a miracle, but every miracle is a parable. By his long all-night delay, and then by his coming to them, Jesus taught his disciples that their interests are ever upon his heart. His Church may struggle in the deep, by heresies distressed, by schisms rent asunder; but at the right hand of God Christ keepeth watch over his own. His disciple may be tossed and driven with the waves, but from his mountaintop he beholds your struggles and observes your trials.

Man craves the knowledge and the sympathy of the Eternal. During a lull between the charges at the second battle of Cold Harbor, in June, 1864, the only battle that Grant said he regretted fighting, officers going through the Union ranks saw the men where they were sitting on the grass under the trees, or in the thickets, sewing their names on the sleeves of their coats. Why were they doing that? It was because they expected to die in the ensuing charge, and shrank from the oblivion of a nameless grave. They wanted someone in the hills of western Pennsylvania, Vermont, New York, Wisconsin, to know how they had died and where and when, and where their bodies rested. Yes, the human heart wants to know if there is any ear to hear, or any eye to witness its sorrows, its conflicts, and its struggles. Christian faith answers that cry; it tells us that there is no place where earth's sorrows are more felt than in heaven, and that, though man is tossed with the winds in the midst of the sea, Christ is watching from his mountaintop.

Sometime ago I received a letter from a woman who had suffered intensely through the death of a much-loved father. With his latest breath he had enjoined her to care tenderly for her sister, a blind and helpless girl. This she has done with great fidelity. Yet she is conscious of great loneliness and sorrow. She wanted to know if God really cared, and if, after all, we could count on the sympathy of Christ. When the letter came I had just been reading Mark's story of the storm that night on the Sea of Galilee, and so my answer was right at hand. I asked her to read the story of the miracle, and especially this verse, "And when even was come, the ship was in the midst of the sea, and he alone on the land. And he saw them toiling in the rowing, for the wind was contrary unto them." There, in the Evangelist's beautiful words, is the assurance that Christ sees, that he knows and cares, and is touched with a feeling for our infirmities.

## Jesus Is Not a Phantom

About the fourth hour, that eerie time when human energy is at its lowest, before the darkness passes into light, Jesus came to them walking on the sea. When the disciples first saw him they were terrified and cried out. To the terrors of the sea and the wind and the night there was now added the terror of the unseen world. But immediately Jesus called out to them, "It is I; be not afraid." When they heard that Voice, they knew that all was well. Jesus is the Voice which speaks through the winds and the waves and elemental commotions of life, letting us know that there is more than blind force and energy at work in the world, that Divine Love is working and planning and ruling. "Let not your heart be troubled: ye believe in God, believe also in me." "It is I; be not afraid."

## Jesus and Peter

Now comes the dramatic incident about Peter which appears only in Matthew's account of the storm. Peter's performance here is altogether in keeping with his unmistakable character. If Mat-

[ 37 ]

thew had told the story without giving the name of the apostle who tried to walk on the sea, we would have had no difficulty in guessing who it was. Peter always had to be in action. In the great and stirring moments of Christ's ministry, here on the sea, on the mount of transfiguration, in the garden of Geth-semane, Peter always wants to do something. He can do anything but sit still or keep still. When he realizes that it is really Jesus, all his fear and doubt vanished, and in triumphant spirit he called out, "Lord, if it be thou, bid me come unto thee on the water." It was not that Peter had any doubt about Christ really being there, but it was as if he had said, "Lord, since it is thou, and since thou hast the power, bid me come unto thee on the water."

If for no other reason, Peter deserves to stand, as he always does, first in the catalogue of the apostles, because of the place he gives to the person and the power of Christ. He believed that Christ was so great that not only could he walk on the sea, but he could make others walk, too. Peter failed in his attempt, as we shall see; but the great thing about him was that he, at least, tried; and far better an effort of faith that fails than a cool and calculating attitude that will take no chances.

In answer to Peter's request Jesus said to him, "Come!" And without a moment's hesitation, Peter stepped over the gunwale of the ship into the sea. For a little all went well—as long as Peter kept his eye fixed upon Christ, and he actually walked on the sea. But when he looked away from Christ, and saw the angry sea, and the white crest of the waves and heard the roaring of the wind, he became afraid, and beginning to sink, cried out, "Lord, save me." This happened because Peter was afraid. A great many things happen when we are afraid. Fear confuses the mind, paralyzes our energy, blots out the goal from our view. When you begin to fear, you begin to sink. How many times we hear Christ say to his disciples, "Fear not; be of good courage."

When Peter cried out, "Lord, save me," immediately Jesus stretched forth his hand and caught him. Peter had failed; but in his failure he called upon Christ to save him. It was a short prayer and a quick answer. "Lord, save me." And immediately Jesus stretched forth his hand and caught him.

Is anyone here today sinking? Sinking into the dark sea of fear, or doubt, or sorrow, or sin? Then do what Peter did. There is the prayer for you—"Lord, save me." "And Jesus stretched forth his hand, and caught him." That Hand has lost none of its power to save. O divine Hand, Hand that rested upon the head of the little children; Hand that touched the tongue of the dumb and it spake; Hand that touched the ear of the deaf and it heard; Hand that touched the ear in the Garden of Gethsemane that Peter had struck off with his sword and restored it; Hand that touched the leper and cleansed him;

Hand that touched the bier on which lay the only **son** of the widow of Nain, and he lived; Hand that caught Peter when he was sinking in the sea; Hand that carried off the gates of death and hell; Hand that was nailed to the cursed tree for our salvation— whenever I am sinking, let me feel thy saving grasp, even as Peter felt it when he was sinking that dark night on the Sea of Galilee.

# PETER'S NEVER-ANSWERED QUESTION

## IV

### *"Lord, to whom shall we go? thou hast the words of eternal life"*

John 6: 68

SOMETIMES you feel like denouncing and reproaching Peter. Other times you feel like cheering him. It is said that the angels rejoice. If so, they may be capable of sorrow also; and if they both rejoice and sorrow, then there is no one over whom the angels must have rejoiced more and sorrowed more than Peter. This is one of those times. The crowds which had been attracted to Christ in his early ministry were beginning to fall away from him. They were more interested in the loaves and fishes which he dispensed than in the Bread of Life that cometh down from heaven. Christ never made the terms of discipleship easy. He never coaxed anyone to join his Church. When he had spoken plain words to the multitude, and plain words to those who had been known as his disciples, "from that time," said John, "many of his disciples went back and walked no more with him." Jesus watched in silence the departure of these "sunshine disciples" who had lost their faith and zeal, and then turning to the Twelve, he said—and there must have been the accent of sorrow in his voice—"Will ye also go away?" Quick as a flash came Peter's beautiful and loyal answer. "Lord, to whom shall we go? thou hast the words of eternal life."

This was a word spoken in season, like "apples of gold in pictures of silver." It was the word that Christ needed to hear just at that moment; and great is the distinction of Peter that from his loyal, loving heart, and from his impulsive lips, came this great declaration and question unanswerable. Peter was speaking out of his own personal experience. "And we believe," he said, "and are sure that thou art that Christ, the Son of the living God."

A test of the value of any given thing is whether or not a substitute can be secured for it. If some other thing will serve just as well, then its value is limited. But if there is no substitute for it, it is of the highest value. That was what Christ meant when he said, "What shall a man give in exchange for his soul?" In all the world there is nothing to take the place of a soul. Peter, stirred by the question of Jesus, impulsively asked, "Lord, to whom shall we go but unto thee? If we leave thee, to whom shall we turn? To the Scribes, to the Pharisees, to the priests, to Herod, to Pilate? If we go from thee, who will take thy place? Who can speak unto us words of eternal life?" With this incident from the ministry of our Lord for a starting point, I would like to show the pre-eminence, exclusiveness, and indispensableness of Christ.

## I

If we forsake Christ as an Example and a Guide, to whom shall we go? Youth reveres and worships personality. It is on the march with a true hero. But what person is like to Christ? Sinless himself, he creates the idea and ideal of a holy life. In the heart of man there is a deep and secret longing for the perfect and complete life, and that longing is confirmed in Christ. Into our world so marred and trampled, and stained, and defiled by the feet of sinners, there came this man who, upon the testimony of angels and devils, of friend and enemy, did no sin. Upon the face of even the fairest and noblest of the sons of men we discern flaws and shadows; but there is no shadow upon the face of Christ.

Such a life, sinless, yet bearing our nature and lived in our midst, becomes our pattern and our guide. Our hearts long for One in whom we can trust implicitly. We cry out for a strength and a wisdom, and an experience beyond our own, beyond that of man. "Lead me to the rock that is higher than I." And there, the same yesterday, today, and forever, is Jesus Christ, the Rock of Ages, the rock higher than I! Christ says to us, "Follow me." Who else could say that? Follow me, in the echo of every public or spoken or printed word; in every highway of act and deed; into every secret chamber of thought and desire and imagination? If you leave Christ as the perfect example, what I want to know is this—to whom will you go? Whom will you take to be your guide? Your heart yearns for the true hero, and here he is, chief of ten thousand, the One altogether lovely. None ever followed him and was disappointed, or deceived, or disillusioned. But thousands upon thousands who have followed him through all the pilgrimage of life are on record as saying what John Bunyan said in those beautiful and incomparable words, "I have loved to hear my Master spoken of, and wherever I have seen the print of his shoe in the earth, there I have coveted to set my foot, too. His name has been to me as a civet box; yea, sweeter than all perfume. And his face I have desired more than the light of the sun. His words I have used to gather food for me and as antidotes against my fainting."

## II

If you leave Christ, your Friend, Companion, and Helper, to whom will you go? We need a goal and a standard, a command and an exhortation; but we need also a Companion, a Comforter, and a Friend; for sometimes we lose the way, or wander from it, tempted by fairer sights and sounds which deceive us; or we stumble over the rocks on the path; or we faint beneath the midday sun; or we are wounded by the arrows of foes in ambush; or the silence and the blackness of the night terrifies us. Thousands of pilgrims are on record as testifying that for all these hours and circumstances the one who could be trusted is Christ. Could any other take his place? If you hear not his voice, then whose voice can speak to you, and whose gentle hand can be laid upon you when your guilty head is low in the dust of remorse and despair; when we lie upon some bed of pain and anguish; when the soul kneels apart in the Gethsemane of its sorrow and woe; when our tears fall hot and fast into the deep and narrow trench of the grave; or when our own feet are going down into the Dark River itself?

You can go to dreamers and reformers and teachers. But what can they say or do? Take such a hymn, for example, as

"What a Friend we have in Jesus,
    All our sins and griefs to bear!
What a privilege to carry
    Everything to God in prayer." [1]

Take that hymn and try to substitute some other name for the name of Jesus. Take the name of Plato, or Socrates, or any of the great sages of the past, or some of the worthies of the Old Testament

[1] Joseph Scriven.

[ 45 ]

—Moses, Elijah, David, Daniel—or the great souls of the New Testament—Peter, James, John, Paul—and make the hymn sing, "What a friend we have in Elijah," "What a friend we have in David," "What a friend we have in Paul, or John"—how cold and lifeless and absurd the hymn becomes. Why? Because there is no substitute for Christ. Or write into the hymn in place of faith in Jesus and prayer unto Him, science, art, wisdom, fame, literature—are they able to bear all your sins and grief? Have they arms into which they can take and shield you? Will you be able to find a solace *there?*

Calling not long ago on an invalid widow, and looking about the living room, I said, "Is this where you sit most of the time?" "No," she said; "I generally sit in the room upstairs. This is the room where my husband used to sit with me. In the room upstairs it does not seem so lonely." How many there are like that lonely woman, seeking to move out of the shadow of life's loneliness! Our friends in the flesh, and in memory, too, how much we owe to them! How could we get along without them? But these friends, one by one, are separated from us. The soul yearns for the Eternal Friend and Companion. What a friend Christ is! If I could borrow this morning Jacob's Ladder, and climb up into heaven and search it through and through, I would not be able to find a friend like Jesus.

"One there is, above all others,
    Well deserves the name of Friend;
His is love beyond a brother's,
    Costly, free, and knows no end;
They who once His kindness prove
Find it everlasting love."

## III

If we leave Christ as the sinner's Saviour, as the only Redeemer from sin, to whom shall we go? Christ, alone, died for sinners. He is the sinner's only substitute; for him there is no substitute.

Let us see what Christ did for us on the Cross. He offered to God his sacrifice of perfect obedience and holiness. None other could make that sinless offering. Since he was the Son of God, he perfectly represented God, and his sacrifice is of infinite value and effect; and since he is the Son of man, he perfectly represents man and is able to carry our sins up to the Cross. There on the Cross he satisfied divine justice, and at the same time opened the gates of eternal mercy and love to the sinner. He reconciles man to God. Through faith in Christ we come to God, not only pardoned, set free from the penalty, but made just. If sin is what the Bible and experience and conscience and history declare it to be, and if sin requires punishment and expiation, atonement and satisfaction, then who can take the place of Christ? Others have claimed to teach or to heal, to lead or to inspire; but who ever claimed to take the place of Christ upon the Cross? In the Garden of Gethsemane, in the midst of his agony, a stone's throw between him and the nearest disciples, Christ prayed, "If it be possible, let this cup pass from me." But, it was not possible! He had to drink the cup and bear the burden of our sins. Do you think that, where God could find no substitute for Christ and his death on the Cross, you will be able to find a substitute?

> "There was no other good enough
>     To pay the price of sin;
> He only could unlock the gate
>     Of heaven, and let us in." [2]

When you stand before the Judgment Seat, who but Christ can answer for you?

## IV

If we leave Christ as the Resurrection and Life, to whom shall we go? Who else has the words of Eternal Life? The last enemy—and what an enemy he is—who can evade him? Who can overcome him, or conquer him? When the children of Israel had finished their forty years' wandering in the wilderness, after all their trials and adversities, after the passage of the Red Sea, and the drought and the plague and the serpents and the Amalekites and the

[2] Mrs. Cecil F. Alexander.

Amorites, they had to meet the final and most difficult trial of all—the river Jordan. So at the end of all our pilgrimage and all our warfare, there flows the cold, dark, sullen stream of death. It matters not what success we have had with our other foes, the great question is—How shall we meet and conquer death? Who will help us over the river? Who will give us a sure conviction that on the other side are the evergreen plains and hills of a life that is free, sinless, eternal? If, at the river of death, you turn from Christ, then what I want to know is this—to whom will you go? To nature? Nature cannot help you.

> "Thou makest thine appeal to me:
>     I bring to life, I bring to death:
>     The spirit does but mean the breath.
> I know no more." [3]

You make your appeal to the philosophers, sages, and the wise men. Some of them say, Yes; some of them say, No. Or after great argument about it they leave you just where you were. All that you have is a vague surmise, a perhaps. Or you turn to human experience. It can speak no accent of hope. Here they come, family after family, company after company, generation after generation, nation after nation—all marching down the steep bank into the

[3] Tennyson, "In Memoriam," LVI. Houghton Mifflin.

dark cold waters of death. We see them go down; we see them disappear from sight—but never again do we behold them emerge. Human experience is all against the idea of immortality and life beyond the grave. By the grave of a little child, Robert Ingersoll said: "We do not know which is the greatest blessing, life or death. We cannot say that death is not good. We do not know whether the grave is the end of life or the door of another, or whether the night here is not somewhere else a dawn. Neither can we tell which is the more fortunate, the child dying in its mother's arms before its lips have learned to form a word, or he who journeys all the length of life's uneven road, painfully taking the last slow steps with staff and crutch. Every cradle asks us, Whence? and every coffin asks us, Whither?"

Beautiful rhetoric; the poetry of speech. But what comfort and what hope is there? But here is One whom we behold go down into the river of death and whom we behold emerge from it again, who not only said, "I am the Resurrection and the Life," but proved it by his own death and resurrection; who said, "Let not your heart be troubled: ye believe in God, believe also in me. I go to prepare a place for you. If it were not so, I would have told you." If you leave this Christ on the shores of death, then to whom will you go?

Michelangelo was an incarnation of the art and learning and wisdom of the Middle Ages. Yet when

he came near to the end of his life, all his art and
culture and learning meant nothing to him, and he
put his trust in Christ and him crucified. He tells
us this in his beautiful sonnet—

"Now hath my life across a stormy sea,
    Like a frail bark, reached that wide port where all
    Are hidden ere the final reckoning fall
Of good and evil for eternity.
Now know I well how that fond fantasy
    Which made my soul the worshiper and thrall
    Of earthly art, is vain: how criminal
Is that which all men seek unwittingly.

Those amorous thoughts which were so lightly dressed,
    What are they when a double death is nigh,
        The one I know for sure, the other dread?
Painting nor sculpture now can lull to rest
    My soul that turns to His great love on High,
        Whose arms to clasp us on the cross were spread."

I may be speaking to some who have followed
Christ, but are now tempted to turn away from him.
Let me say this to you. Before you abandon Christ
and turn from him, be sure that you have someone to
take his place. You may have had doubts sown in
your mind by some book that you have read, by some
address you have heard, by some disloyal utterance
or act of a professed follower of Christ, or some
statement by a proud scholar or scientist; but before
you leave Christ, ask yourself Peter's question,

"Lord, to whom shall I go? thou hast the words of eternal life." Perhaps I am speaking to some who have not yet followed Christ, who have not taken him as King, Redeemer, Saviour, and Lord. If so, whom will you follow? If you will not come to Christ, then what I want to know is this—to whom will you go?

No doubt I speak to one who once followed Christ, and then forsook him. To you I say, remember Peter's experience. He followed and then forsook Christ. But he came back again; he came back with tears of repentance. He tried to answer his own question and failed. No one can answer it. There is no other to whom we can go.

# PETER'S LESSON ON FORGIVENESS

## V

### *"Until seventy times seven"*

Matthew 18: 22

IN his *Rise of the Dutch Republic*, Motley relates an incident of the days of the persecution of the Protestants. One of the Catholic persecutors was pursuing a Protestant across a frozen lake, when the ice broke and he was plunged into the water. The fleeing Protestant, hearing his cries, turned back and rescued him from a watery grave. But as soon as they reached the land the heartless persecutor seized him and delivered him over to his enemies, who burned him at the stake.

Our Lord's parable of the heartless debtor reveals a harshness and a lack of mercy like that of the Catholic persecutor who committed to the flames the man who had rescued him from drowning. But there was this difference. The monstrous persecutor was under the spell of a religious fanaticism; whereas this cruel ingrate in the parable of Jesus could plead no such extenuation.

Our Lord had been speaking to his disciples on the

[ 53 ]

subject of forgiveness, and how to be reconciled to those who have offended us. Then Peter broke in with his question—"Lord, how oft shall my brother sin against me, and I forgive him? till seven times?" Jesus answered, "I say not unto thee, Until seven times: but, Until seventy times seven." When Peter set the standard at seven times, he thought he was making a very liberal allowance; and, indeed, he had gone much beyond the custom of his day. But Jesus tells him that the standard is not seven times, but until seventy times seven; that is, there is to be no limit to one's forgiveness of another. Peter was going to reduce it to a code; but Jesus lifts the whole subject into the realm of the spirit.

In order to illustrate his point, Jesus tells the parable of the Unmerciful Servant. "The kingdom of heaven is like unto a certain king who demanded a reckoning from his servants." Always in the background of life there is the shadow of that reckoning the thought of which ought to have real influence upon our conduct now, the day of examination and of judgment. That day may dawn as suddenly and unexpectedly as it did for this dishonest and unmerciful servant.

This servant was very likely the ruler of a province, a sort of Oriental satrap. This would explain his enormous debt of ten thousand talents, amounting to millions of dollars. He had been squandering the revenues, and now he is asked to square his accounts. He has nothing with which to pay the debt, and by the law of the land he and his family could be sold into slavery. Indeed, that order had already been given. The despairing and dishonest debtor fell down before his lord and cried out, "Lord, have patience with me, and I will pay thee all." That he knew, and his lord too, was an impossibility. The stealings and the pillage of a lifetime could not be made good in the few years of life now left to this debtor. How could he get together millions of dollars with a jail sentence hanging over him? It was preposterous. But his lord had compassion on him, and not only suspended the sentence, but forgave him the debt.

We would like to think that this debtor, after he had embraced his lord and thanked him in the eloquent language of tears, hurried off to his house and told his wife and children that through the great mercy and goodness of their lord they were not to be cast out of their home and sold into slavery, for his whole debt had been forgiven him by his gracious master. Instead of that, what happened? As he passed out of the palace the forgiven servant encountered one of his fellow servants who owed him a hundred shillings, about seventeen dollars. The million-dollar debtor who had been forgiven took this man by the throat, and with brutal threats, shaking him, said, "Pay me what thou owest!" The unhappy man made the same prayer that the unmerciful servant had made but a moment before to his lord, "Have patience with me, and I will pay thee all." But this time the prayer fell on unheeding ears. He who had just been forgiven the enormous debt, with a heart of iron cast into prison the man who owed him the sum of seventeen dollars.

Now comes a turn in the parable which is sometimes overlooked; that is, the witness and the protest of outraged justice in the breast of man. The spirit of justice and right cannot be altogether silenced or suppressed. A wicked monstrous thing had been done, but when the man's fellow servants heard of it they were sorry and went and told their lord what had happened. It's one thing to feel sorry for those who have suffered wrong or injustice, but it is another thing, not only to feel sorry, but to do something for them. These men were not only moved, but they acted upon their emotion. They were sorry; but when their lord heard of it he was angry. Summoning the heartless, wicked servant, he said to him, "O thou wicked servant, I forgave thee all that debt, because thou desiredst me: shouldest not thou also have compassion on thy fellow servant, even as I had pity on thee?" And his lord was wroth, and delivered him to the tormentors, till he should pay all that was due unto him.

Then Christ drew the lesson of this great story which had been suggested by Peter's question as to how many times he ought to forgive his brother:

"So likewise shall my heavenly Father do also unto you, if ye from your hearts forgive not every one his brother their trespasses."

If you took out of the New Testament the questions that Peter asked and the answers that Jesus gave him, how great would be our loss! In this answer which he gave to Peter's question, Jesus declares the beauty and strength of forgiveness on one side, and on the other the danger, the guilt, and the misery of an unforgiving spirit.

## I. FORGIVENESS THE DISTINCTIVE THING IN CHRISTIAN MORALITY AND ETHICS

The great thing in our Christian religion is redemption from sin. In his infinite mercy God pardons and restores the sinner on the ground of Christ's plea and sacrifice on the Cross. It is not strange, therefore, that on the side of Christian morals and ethics the thing which is most emphasized and most distinctive in Christian teaching is man's forgiveness of man. In this parable, and elsewhere, it is taught that a necessary result of the acceptance of God's mercy and forgiveness in Christ must be the spirit of forgiveness toward one another. The Apostle Paul phrases it in this beautiful way: "Forgiving one another, even as God for Christ's sake hath forgiven you."

The problem of enmity, offense, and an unforgiving spirit as a real obstacle to the work of the Holy

Spirit must be a very serious problem, else Christ would not have spoken so frequently upon this subject. Here the teaching of Jesus is unique and distinctive. On almost every other subject what he says in regard to human conduct can be paralleled by teachings in the Old Testament. But when he comes to this subject of forgiveness, of injuries, Christ is remote not only from the world of pagan and heathen thought and action, but from the law and custom of the old dispensation. There are indeed in the Old Testament beautiful foregleams of the teachings of Jesus, and men who were Christians before Christ, like Joseph, who forgave his brethren; or David, who forgave Saul his cruel persecution and injustice; but, as a clear and definite law, the world had to wait until Christ opened the volume of the New Testament. How true this is, that Christ's teaching of forgiveness of one another is the distinctive thing in Christian ethics, is shown by the way men speak of the Christian spirit. When you say that a man has a Christian spirit, what do you mean? You do not mean that he is generous; you do not mean that he is hopeful; you do not mean that he is sympathetic; you do not mean that he is a man of integrity; you do not mean that he is courageous. What you mean, when you say a man has a Christian spirit, is that he is enough of a Christian, enough Christlike, to forgive an injury. In Seeley's beautiful paraphrase

[ 58 ]

of the New Testament in *Ecce Homo*, "And God said, Let there be light, and there was forgiveness."

## II. CHRIST TEACHES NOT ONLY FORGIVENESS, BUT RECONCILIATION

This means much more than forgiveness. He does not say merely, "Overlook and pay no regard to the injury you have received. To take vengeance will only injure you. After all, the world is big enough for two people who are alienated to move in it without colliding with one another"; but he says that we are to seek reconciliation. "Thou hast gained thy brother"—that was the great objective that Christ had in mind.

Not only did Christ say that this was desirable, but he says that the spirit that makes the effort toward reconciliation possible is necessary before acceptable worship and before pardon. "If thou bring thy gift to the altar, and there rememberest that thy brother hath aught against thee; leave there thy gift before the altar, and . . . first be reconciled to thy brother, and then come and offer thy gift."

In advising Christians at Corinth, after they had disciplined an unworthy member of the Church, to forgive him and restore him, Paul adds this significant warning: "Lest Satan have an advantage over you." It might be put this way: "Lest Satan get a grip or a hold on you." Satan knows he has a great advantage and a great chance over a soul when he can persuade the soul to keep enmity or hatred toward another. The question is sometimes asked as to what believing Christians are going to do when they meet enemies in heaven. The shortest answer to that question is that enemies will not meet in heaven. Enmity in the heart toward a fellow man will bar the soul from heaven. How can an unforgiving soul breathe the pure atmosphere of the Kingdom of God?

One of the most charming of the older American homes is the Hermitage, not far from Nashville, Tenn. The estate lies in the midst of fertile rolling country, well watered like the Garden of the Lord. Between rows of stately cedars the driveway leads up to the lawn in the front of the mansion, which is of heavy, yet simple, colonial style, and much more imposing than either Mount Vernon, or Jefferson's mountain home, Monticello. On the May day when I visited the Hermitage, with the mockingbirds and bulfinches pouring out their songs in springtime melody, with all the hills and meadows clothed in their unwoven garment of tender green, and the sheep and cattle and horses browsing or leaping in the fields, it seemed to me it was about as near to an earthly paradise as one could find, did he search the world around. There the stern old soldier lived for wellnigh half a century, and there in a modest sepulcher, instead of in the sarcophagus of the Roman Emperor Alexander Severus which an American Commodore had offered him, and which now may be seen in the

Museum in Fairmount Park at Philadelphia, he sleeps by the side of his beloved wife who brought so much joy and so much pain into his stormy career. The last words of the chaste epitaph which Jackson himself wrote for his wife refers to the slanders from which his wife has suffered: "A being so gentle and so virtuous, slander might wound, but could not dishonor; and even Death, when he bore her from the arms of her husband, could but transport her to the bosom of her God."

On a plot of ground across the road from the Hermitage stands a little brick church which Jackson built for the convenience of his wife, who was as pious as she was beautiful. He had solemnly promised his wife that when he was done with politics he would unite with the Church. It was not, however, until 1842, three years before his death, that he made a profession of Christian faith. The reason he gave for the long delay was the fear lest his political enemies should say that he had joined the Church for political effect. Fourteen years after the death of his wife he took the Communion and was received into the Presbyterian Church.

When the minister was examining him as to his faith and experience, he asked him a question that probably not many ministers would have asked him. He said: "General, there is one more question which it is my duty to ask you. Can you forgive all your enemies?" The question was in view of the many feuds, duels, and personal bitternesses of Jackson's stormy career. After a moment's silence, Jackson responded: "My political enemies I can freely forgive; but as for those who abused me when I was serving my country in the field, and those who attacked me for serving my country, and those who slandered my wife . . . doctor, that is a different case." The minister made it clear to him that none who willfully harbored ill feelings against a fellow being could make a sincere profession of faith. Again there was silence, until at length the aged candidate affirmed that he would try to forgive all his enemies. This done, his name was written upon the rolls of the church and he received the Communion of the Body and Blood of Christ.

Forgiveness brings to men the joy and peace of the heavenly life. In the National Gallery in London, among the paintings before which one likes to pause the longest are those by the eighteenth-century artist, George Romney. He is the artist who painted Emma Hart, afterwards celebrated as Lord Nelson's friend, Lady Hamilton. She became the model from whom he worked constantly, painting her as Magdalene, Joan of Arc, as Circe, a Bacchante, and a Cassandra. In 1756 Romney married a young woman who nursed him through a fever. Afterwards he deserted her because someone had told him that marriage was fatal to a successful career as an artist. Years afterwards, broken in health and spirit, and half demented, he returned to his wife, who nursed him with unchanged affection and beautiful, heaven-like forgiveness.  In the prayer which Tennyson puts into Romney's mouth, the contrite artist, says:

> "O yes, I hope, or fancy that perhaps
>   Human forgiveness touches heaven, and thence—
> For you forgive me, you are sure of that—
> Reflected, sends a light on the forgiven." [1]

There is no question about that.  Forgiveness is the reflected light of heaven.  It lights up the countenance of him that is forgiven and of him who forgives.

> "It is twice blessed;
> It blesses him that gives, and him that takes."

I wish that I could have been there when Jesus, in answer to Peter's question, "How many times shall I forgive my brother?" said, "Not until seven times, but until seventy times seven."  I am sure that there was a tone in the voice of Christ, and a look in his eye which must have startled Peter.  Perhaps he said to himself, "Why does the Master look at me in that way?"

One day Peter was to learn the meaning of that look in Christ's face, that arresting accent in his

---

[1] Cambridge Edition.  Published by Houghton Mifflin Company.

voice. It was the night in which he was betrayed and in which he was denied. Peter with a loud oath has denied for the third time that he is a disciple of Jesus, or that he ever knew him, and just as his loud oath is ringing through the courtyard, Jesus, his hands bound and his face bleeding from the blows which had been inflicted upon him in the judgment chamber of Caiaphas, is led out into the hallway. As he heard Peter's oath, he turned and looked upon him. And it was a look of infinite forgiveness. Now Peter knows why Christ looked so earnestly on him that day long before when he said to him, "Until seventy times seven."

# PETER'S FEET

## VI

### *"He took a towel"*

John 13: 4

#### (A COMMUNION MEDITATION)

ONCE, on a fair August Sabbath, I drove from Harper's Ferry across the Potomac to Paradise Valley on the Maryland side. Paradise Valley is pleasantly named, and on that beautiful summer Sabbath seemed not unworthy of its name. Seeing a Dunkard Church on the hillside, I stopped to worship at the rural temple. But the service was just concluding and the congregation was coming out of the doors. Strong, rugged, honest-looking country folk they were. Falling into conversation with one of the leading men, I asked him about some of their practices, and particularly concerning the rite of foot washing. "Why," I asked, "did they maintain this practice?" His answer was that the washing of feet was one of the things that Christ did at the Lord's Supper, and the meaning of which he was careful to impress on his disciples. That, he thought, was reason enough, for the followers of Christ to wash one another's feet when they celebrated the sacrament. But, in addition to that, he said it was good and wholesome for a rich man to wash a poor man's feet, or a poor man a rich man's feet; or a man who was estranged from his neighbor to wash his feet.

Strange, that in this wonderful Gospel of St. John, which was written, as he says, to the end that men might believe that Christ was the Son of God, and where almost half of the twenty-one chapters are devoted to the last twenty-four hours of the life of Jesus, there should be two chapters, one after the other, the twelfth and the thirteenth, in which the chief incident related has to do with feet. In the twelfth chapter we have the story of how Mary anointed the feet of Jesus and wiped them with her hair. In the thirteenth chapter we have the story of how Christ washed the feet of his disciples and wiped them with a towel.

St. John, who leaned on Christ's breast that night, gives us the fullest account of what transpired. To him we owe the record of Christ's tender valedictory, when he said, "Let not your heart be troubled"; and the record of his sublime intercessory prayer; and the story of how he washed the disciples' feet; and the fullest account of Judas on that last night. Yet, singularly enough, John left no record of the actual institution of the Lord's Supper. Perhaps when he came to write his Gospel, which was the latest of all the Gospels, he felt that he could not improve on what the others had said, and recorded things which they had omitted in the story of that night of nights.

The disciples were having a quarrel as to who should be accounted the greatest. In the intensity of their dispute, it seems that either they, or the master of the house, had neglected the ordinary Oriental courtesy, and had supplied no water for the washing of feet. This gave Jesus his chance. They wanted to know who was greatest, and how to rise to pre-eminence. He would show them. He took a towel and girded himself and began to wash the disciples' feet.

What an incomparable scene for the painter, with words or with colors! Perhaps he commenced with John, who was probably at his right, and so went round the circle of the disciples—John, then Matthew, and Thomas, and Philip, and Bartholomew, and the rest of them. We can imagine the look of astonishment and perhaps embarrassment and shame, which came over the countenances of the disciples as Jesus bent before them to wash their feet. And now he comes to Judas! We wonder if he whispered to Judas a last appeal to turn back from the treachery which was leading him into outer darkness. But the touch of the hands of Jesus upon the feet of Judas made no impression. Thomas de Quincey, writing on Judas Iscariot, said he would like to look into the face of the man who, having dipped his hand in the same dish with the Son of Man, could afterwards betray him. But if Judas with his hand in the dish with the Son of Man is a mystery, what shall we say of Judas who, unmoved, permits Jesus to wash his feet?

When the feet of the last disciple had been washed, Jesus put his outer garment on again and resumed his place at the table.

It had been a great acted parable; but lest any of them should miss the meaning, Christ said that he had left them an example, that they should do as he had done and wash one another's feet. They called him Master and Lord, and he had proved his right to the title by this lowly act of service. They ought to follow in his steps, and, if they did so, they would find happiness. "If ye know these things, happy are ye if ye do them."

The beautiful scene at the Supper on that last night is the Bible's greatest sermon on humility. There are two chief aspects of humility—humility toward our fellow men, and humility in our attitude toward God. Take, first, humility toward others.

He took a towel! He might have taken anything that he wanted. He might have taken a scepter; he might have taken a crown; he might have taken the throne of the world's dominion; he might have taken the sword of a conqueror; but instead of that the Lord of Glory took a towel.

Christ did not demean himself when he stooped to

wash the disciples' feet. Never does his stature seem so great as when he bent over the feet of his friends. What an example that is to us, and what a rebuke to our strivings, our insistence on right and place and recognition. Humility—born, like that of Christ, of love—avoids strife, silences abuse and criticism, vaunteth not itself, is not puffed up, and shows us how not to think more highly of ourselves than we ought to think. Humility is the fountain of generosity, for it is easy to give that which we have ceased to regard as our own.

How much of life's friction and strife and bitterness would be avoided, if men walked Christ's path of humility.

Here, too, is the secret of happiness. "Ye ought to wash one another's feet," said Christ; "and, if ye do this, happy are ye." The true blessedness and the inner happiness are found in obedience to this law of humility. How true it is that our deepest satisfactions, our happiest moments, have come, not from the assertion of self, nor the recognition and honor of ourselves by others, but from deeds of helpfulness and kindness and sympathy which we have done for others. Men seek far afield for life's blessedness and happiness, imagining that it must be found in doing some great and unusual thing; but Christ tells us that it is found nearer home. Few can wave the wand of the poet or the orator; few can wear the mantle of the true statesman, or trace the golden letters of the scholar; but anyone can take a towel. Towels are cheap, and so is water; and weary, dusty feet are always on our borders.

The other aspect of humility is humility toward God. "Walk humbly with thy God." In its highest form, humility is the soul's acceptance of the gift of forgiveness through our Lord Jesus Christ.

It was Peter's protest that night which gave Jesus his opportunity to explain the symbolic meaning of this beautiful act of washing the disciples' feet. When he came to Peter, Peter, just as you might have expected, exclaimed in amazement and protest, "Lord, dost thou wash my feet?" Jesus gave him an answer which will ever mean much to us in the day of trial and trouble, but which Peter missed entirely: "What I do thou knowest not now, but thou shalt know hereafter." Not to be put off with an answer like that, Peter exclaimed in his impulsive, boasting, and yet always engaging manner, "Lord, thou shalt never wash my feet!" That gave Christ his chance. Immediately came his great answer, "If I wash thee not, thou hast no part with me." Then Peter went, as usual, to the other extreme; and seeing what Christ meant, exclaimed, "Lord, not my feet only, but also my hands and my head." It was the prayer of the Psalmist over again, "Wash me thoroughly from my sin, and cleanse me from mine iniquity."

Christ commenced this great sermon and parable of washing the disciples' feet to teach them humility toward one another, and to inspire them to help and to serve one another. It accomplished that great end. What Christ did they did not know then; but now, hereafter, we know, for when he stooped that night to wash the disciples' feet, Christ was founding hospitals, asylums, orphan homes, and starting in motion that river of compassion which has been flowing through the scorched, sin-smitten fields of humanity ever since.

But on that night Christ taught a greater lesson than humility and love to one another. The protest of Peter gave him his chance to say, under the most impressive circumstances, that if Christ does not wash the sinner, he can have no part with him. Now, it takes humility, humility born of the Holy Spirit, to accept that truth. And what is it that we all need? That we need to be instructed, that we need to be led, that we need to be developed, that we need to be inspired—all this is true. But to accept it as truth, and to look to Jesus Christ for that alone, requires no humility. But to own and confess that our greatest need is to be washed, to be cleansed, and that Christ only can do it—that takes humility.

Some who reject Christ as the Saviour from sin defend and excuse that rejection by quoting that great verse from the book of Micah, "What doth the Lord require of thee, but to do justly, and to love mercy, and to walk humbly with thy God?" Not faith in a Crucified Redeemer, they say, but the life of mercy, justice, and humility is what God requires. But the supreme test of humility toward God is the attitude of the soul toward the Cross of Christ. Let our prayer this morning be, "Lord, not my feet only, but also my hands and my head."

> "Nothing in my hand I bring;
> Simply to Thy Cross I cling;
> Naked, come to Thee for dress;
> Helpless, look to Thee for grace;
> Foul, I to the Fountain fly:
> Wash me, Saviour, or I die." [1]

[1] Augustus M. Toplady.

# CHRIST'S PRAYER FOR PETER

## VII

*"But I have prayed for thee, that
thy faith fail not"*

Luke 22: 32

A WOMAN once said to
me that there was no one in the world who prayed
for her. If so, that was all the more reason why
she needed to pray for herself. Certainly it was
true that she had been prayed for at one time when
she came into the world, and a father's and a mother's
love blended in a spoken or unspoken prayer. There
is not a person here tonight for whom someone in
heaven, on earth, perhaps in hell, has not prayed.
This invests life with a sacred interest.

All through that long, dark night when Peter
slept on his watch in Gethsemane, while the drops of
agony distilled upon his Master's brow; when he
followed Christ afar off; when he sat with his enemies
at the fire to see the end; when his cruel words of
denial rang out in the hall of Caiaphas, and he heard
the awful crow of the cock, and saw Jesus turn to
look upon him, and when he went out into the night

[ 73 ]

to weep bitterly—all through that long, terrible night, there was one faithful friend who went out with him into the blackest night and darkness, down with him into the lowest pit of remorse, and that friend was the prayer of Jesus. Like a star in the heavens over the storm-tossed mariner, that prayer of Jesus shone through the darkness of Peter's night and brought him back at length to the haven of God's love, strengthened, forgiven, converted, and ready to strengthen his brethren.

There was nothing peculiar in the case of Peter. Satan desired to have him, and he desires to have you. In this combat between Satan and the prayer of Christ, Christ's prayer won the battle. In your hour of crisis and temptation, you will find strength in prayer; and not only in prayer, but in the very recollection of the prayers which have been made for your soul.

## I. Our Own Prayers

One of the master touches of a great artist in literature is when he is able to carry a man back to his childhood and have the innocent child of yesterday plead with the hardened sinner of today. The familiar words.

"Backward, turn backward, O Time, in thy flight!
Make me a child again, just for tonight!" [1]

[1] Elizabeth Akers Allen.  Houghton Mifflin Company.

[ 74 ]

are expressive of the belief in the subduing effect of
the recollection of the innocence and happiness of
childhood days.

In his "Snowbound," Whittier imagines a man in
the midst of the great city, and surrounded by its
temptations, being carried back to the scenes of his
boyhood, and the softening and purifying effect which
that memory has upon his heart:

> "Yet, haply, in some lull of life,
>   Some truce of God which breaks its strife,
>   The worlding's eyes shall gather dew,
>     Dreaming in throngful city ways
>   Of winter joys his boyhood knew." [2]

The same master touch is felt in Charles Kingsley's
*Hypatia,* where Philammon goes to the old witch,
Miriam, for a charm with which he can bring Hypatia
to do his will. "The witch draws from her bosom a
broken talisman, at which she looked long and lov-
ingly, kissed it and wept over it, and fondled it in
her arms as a mother with a child. Her grim, withered features grew softer, purer, grander, and rose
ennobled for a moment to their long-lost might-have-
been, to that personal ideal which every soul brings
with it into the world, which shines dim and potential
in the face of every sleeping babe, before it has been
scarred and distorted and incrusted in the long

[2] Cambridge Edition.  Houghton Mifflin Company.

tragedy of life. Sorceress she was, panderer and slave dealer, steeped to the lips in falsehood, ferocity, and avarice, yet that paltry stone brought home to her some thought, true, spiritual, impalpable, un-marketable, before which all her treasures and all her ambitions were as worthless in her own eyes as they were in the eyes of the angels of God." The broken talisman had brought before the wicked woman's mind the vision of another and earlier and an innocent self.

In Thomas More's beautiful tale, the spirit that had been banished from Heaven was told that she could gain entrance there when she brought to its gates the gift most dear to Heaven. She brought first the last drop of blood from a dying patriot's heart; but the gates did not open. She brought then a maiden's kiss of sacrificial love implanted on the brow of her dying lover; but still the gates opened not. Then, near the ruins of Baalbek, she saw a little child kneeling in prayer by a fountain. As the child prayed, a man, on whose face was stamped all iniquity and sin, rode up on his horse, and dismounting, knelt to quench his thirst at the fountain. But as he stooped to lift up the water, he saw the praying child. In a moment the hard face softened, and changed, and a tear flowed down his cheek, for he recalled the day when he, too, was as innocent as the child, and prayed for himself as the child prayed.

Yes, great is the power of recollected prayer, for it may bring the tears of penitence and the sigh of contrition. Perhaps it was the prayer of childhood days, or of one of those sacramental moments, when we were easily affianced to all that is high and good and glorious in life; or when a shaft of pain tore its way through your breast; or when insurgent passions drew you on; or when, in some solitary Gethsemane, with a stone's throw between you and the nearest and dearest, you knelt before your cup and cried, "If it be possible, let this cup pass from me." Or when you lay sick, and so close to the other world that you could feel its cool breath blowing on your brow, and there made your covenant with God.

It was the thought of the prayer of his youth that brought Jacob to repentance and to the favor of God. When he was fleeing from his father's house and his brother's wrath to Padan-aram, and had his dream of the angels and the ladder at that lonely spot on the desert, Jacob put up the stone on which his head had rested for a pillar and, kneeling there, made his vow that if God were faithful to him, and brought him again to his father's land and his father's house, he would come there and worship. But years passed over the head of Jacob before he returned. He had won his battle with the world, and had become a great and prosperous man. But he had not seen much of the angels. When he came back to Canaan, instead of going to Bethel to worship, he settled down to the lush pastures of Shechem, where his whole family sank into idolatry. Then, one day the voice of God spoke: "Arise, go up to Bethel, and dwell there: and make there an altar unto God, that appeared unto thee when thou fleddest from the face of Esau thy brother." Striking his tents, Jacob made the long journey back to Bethel, where, when he had kneeled and offered his sacrifice, God appeared unto him again. When we go back to the altar of prayer that once we built unto the Lord, then God appears again to us and the sacred and holy things of life come back to view.

If only I could bring some of you back to the place where you once prayed for your soul, I would have preached for you the best possible sermon. If now you are tempted, discouraged, disheartened, inclined to give up the battle, and just drift with the tide; or if you are covered with shame and remorse because of recent transgressions and failure, remember how once you prayed for yourself, that in such an hour as is now striking for your soul, your faith might not fail. Oh, hear the earnest whisper of that self of yesterday, speaking to the self of today, "But I have prayed for thee!"

## II. The Prayers of Others

When the Seventh Seal had been opened, an angel came down with a golden censer and offered with much incense the prayers of the saints upon the golden altar, and they went up to God. Life's golden altar is the altar of intercession. Man never does a nobler act than when he becomes a priest to his fellow man and makes intercession for others.

What could be finer than that final touch which Thackeray gives to the beautiful character of Amelia in *Vanity Fair:* "No more fighting was heard at Brussels. The sound of battle rolled miles away. Darkness came down on the field and city, and Amelia was praying for George, who was lying on his face dead, with a bullet through his heart." Sorrow, anguish, battles, wounds, darkness and death; but shining in that darkness the calm star of a faithful woman's intercession!

St. Paul strikes you as a super-Christian: such fortitude in pain and woe, such ability to defy the confederated powers of darkness, and, in spite of deepest affliction or affection, to be governed only by sense of duty; able to fight with beasts at Ephesus, or to languish in a Roman dungeon, and give thanks to God. Surely here is a man who will not feel the need of prayers from others. He can strengthen us, and pray for us, but will not need them himself. But when I go through his letters, I see that he is ever asking his friends—the slaves, artisans, the peasants of Ephesus, Philippi, Thessalonica, Corinth, Rome—to pray for him, that he may have all boldness in utterance for Christ, that great and effectual doors may be opened for him, and that he may never become a castaway. If Paul needed the prayers of others, how much more do we and those by whose side we live.

The greatest prayer that one can offer for another is a prayer for his eternal salvation. A distinguished minister of the Presbyterian Church relates how he had often heard his father pray in church, at the family altar, and at the family table; but it was only when he heard him praying aloud on his knees in the barn that he knew the reality of prayer, and the deep reality of the religious life. And another minister has related how for him a treasured memory was hearing his father on his knees in the barn when the horses were being fed, praying for his soul's salvation. Man reaches his noblest stature when he prays for others. She has long since gone to her reward; but my mind now runs back to the old home on the banks of the river, and I can see the room which was her trysting place with God, and where at a certain hour of the forenoon she was wont to kneel in intercession for the salvation of her children. Truly our mother's works do follow her, now that she herself rests from her labors; and not the least potent and the least blessed among those works is the daily influence of her prayers on our behalf. No rude clamor of the world can altogether dim the sweet reverberation of her prayers in the minds of her children; and if the base solicitations of the world should ever be heeded and obeyed by her children, it will be in spite of, and not for the lack of, a mother's earnest prayers.

In Dick's *Philosophy of a Future State*, the book which converted David Livingstone, there is preserved a beautiful prayer made by a Mrs. Sheppard, a lady of Somersetshire, for the conversion of Lord Byron. In the prayer she referred to him as one as much distinguished for his neglect of God as for the transcendent talents God had bestowed upon him. She prayed that he might be awakened to a sense of his danger and led to seek peace and forgiveness in Christ. After his wife's death, the husband forwarded the prayer to Byron. It took him in one of his best moods, and he responded, "I can assure you that not all the fame which ever cheated humanity into higher notions of its own importance would ever weigh in my mind against the pure and pious interest which a virtuous being may be pleased to take in my behalf. In this point of view, I would not exchange the prayer of the deceased in my behalf for the united glory of Homer, Caesar, and Napoleon."

When we speak of the power of the prayers of others, we must give the first place, next to the sacred prayers of Christ himself, to the prayers of a godly mother. Dr. McCosh, the president of Princeton, fourth back, had a custom of praying with members of the senior class ere he bade them farewell as they went out into the world. When he asked this young man to kneel and pray with him, the man responded that he did not believe in God and did not believe in prayer. Hurt and astonished, Dr. McCosh shook hands with him and bade him farewell. Some years afterwards, he was delivering a course of lectures in Cincinnati. Before going to the lecture hall, he was sitting in the exchange of the hotel when a man came and sat down beside him and said: "What is this, Dr. McCosh, I hear about your turning out infidels at Princeton?" Surprised, Dr. McCosh asked him what he meant. He then gave the history of the student who had refused to pray with Dr. McCosh, saying that he had advanced to an important post in the schools in the city of Cincinnati, and that everywhere he was sowing the seeds of unbelief and infidelity. "But," the man added, "he has a godly, praying mother, and I believe that in the end she will win." A year or two later, Dr. McCosh was in his study at Princeton, when a young man appeared with his wife. He said to Dr. McCosh: "You do not remember me, but I am the student who refused to let you pray with him. I thought that I was an unbeliever, and wherever I could, I sowed the seeds of unbelief, but all the time my godly mother was praying for me. Her prayers have won. I am here in Princeton to enter the Theological Seminary, and before I go I want you to kneel down with me and offer that long-postponed prayer."

When a man enters into battle with the prayers of a godly mother, he is contending with a greater power than we may imagine. There are two things hard to reconcile; the earnest, effectual, fervent, unfailing prayer of a mother, and the eternal loss of that soul for whom the mother has prayed. We accept the statement the Bishop of Hippo made to Monica, the mother of Augustine, when he was annoyed by her importunity in behalf of her wayward, unbelieving son: "Woman, go thy way. It cannot be that a son of so many tears and so many prayers should be lost."

When Christ warned Peter of his fall, and told him that he would pray for him, he said: "I have prayed for thee, that thy faith fail not." A mother, speaking to me recently about a son who has undergone a great trial, asked me to write to him and encourage him, because she feared that his faith might fail. That is the greatest disaster which can overcome a soul. Peter fell and sinned, but his faith did not fail. He never lost his grip on Christ, and when he was converted he strengthened his brethren. This will always remind us that sometimes those who are closest to the recollection of their sins and faults are the ones who can best of all help and strengthen their brethren. When Peter had been forgiven and restored, Christ said to him: "Feed my sheep." All that Christ did for Peter he does for you. He prays for you that your faith shall not fail. When that prayer has been answered, and answered, too, by the obedience of our own will, then God can use us to strengthen the faith and establish the lives of others.

If some of you have stopped praying for yourselves, if no soft light from the prayer of childhood shines on your path, there is one who prays for you. You may have put yourself against yourself; you may have become your own great enemy; but somewhere, someone has carried your name before the throne of grace and mercy; someone has prayed for you in your darkest, hardest hour. Let that Voice now speak to you and cheer you: "But I have prayed for thee!"

### III. The Prayer of Christ

There is nothing in the whole Gospel history of Christ which brings him so near to us, to our weakness, our dangers, our necessities, as this great record that Christ prayed for Peter. It seems to interpret for us the mystery of his Incarnation, his Atonement, and his Resurrection. All these mighty acts were for us and for the welfare of our souls. When we see Christ praying for us, we know what he means. Our nearest and dearest friends come and go, and many a man, when a parent or close friend has died, feels a wave of loneliness sweep over him, as he remembers that he can no longer know that in this life, at least, he has every day the prayers of that faithful friend. But this Friend, Jesus

Christ, ever lives to make intercession for us! His death, if that were possible, but goes to increase the pathos and intensity of his prayers on our behalf.

If Christ prayed for Peter, it was because Peter was worth praying for. The prayers of Christ and the death of Christ are one in this, that they show the value of the human soul. How sad, how sad the contrast; Christ on the cross, Christ in Gethsemane, Christ in heaven, praying and making intercession for the souls of men, and men trying in every possible way by unbelief, by pride, by love, by hate, by enmity, by cruelty, to destroy their own souls and cast them as rubbish to the void! What a contrast! Oh, if anything will arrest you in your fatal course, if anything will bring you to yourself and make you start, ere it is too late, on the long journey to your Father's home, will it not be the recollection of the prayers of Christ? You may have long ceased to pray. Even your own mother may have given you up in her prayers; but Christ still prays for you; still he would bring you to God, if you will but repent and come. Though all things are against you, Christ is for you! May these words never cease to echo and re-echo in your heart, until that heart belongs to God—these holy, sacred, sad, wonderful, beautiful words: "But I, I who suffered, I who died for thee on Calvary, I, the Eternal Son of God, have prayed for thee!"

# A FAR-OFF PETER

## VIII

### *"And Peter followed afar off"*

Luke 22: 54

(A COMMUNION MEDITATION)

WE can learn more from Peter for instruction and warning in our Christian life than from any other of the Apostles; and more on this last night than at any other time of his life.

In the Garden of Gethsemane Peter lay down and slept, together with James and John, while Jesus knelt in his bitter agony. Perhaps no incident or moment in the life and passion of our Lord so brings out the pathos of his loneliness as the sleep of these three disciples. Bad enough for James and John, but worst of all for Peter, because of his fervent boasts and promises that he would be faithful to Jesus when all others forsook him. This no doubt is the reason why, when Jesus came to waken the disciples and remonstrate with them, it was to Peter that he addressed himself, "Simon, sleepest thou? couldst thou not watch one hour?"

When the crisis came, it looks as if Peter would

make good his boast of courage and fidelity. Peter
was no man for the silent vigil. He slept while his
Lord agonized, but when Judas and the band under
the priests and the scribes crowded about his Master
and handled him roughly, Peter could not stand it;
and, drawing his sword, aimed a mighty blow at the
nearest one to him, who happened to be Malchus,
the servant of the High Priest. The blow was not
true, for if it had been, it would have split the man's
head. As it was, it cut off his ear and left a ghastly
mutilation. Jesus healed the wound and, turning to
Peter, rebuked him for his violence and told him to
sheathe his sword. If he wanted a sword, there were
legions of angels whom he could call to defend him.

When the procession started for the judgment
hall of Caiaphas, torches flickering in the night, and
the hoarse voices and murmur of the mob echoing
in the Valley of the Kedron, Peter followed afar off.
That has its good side, in that Peter, aside from
John, seems to have been the only one who followed
Jesus that night. All the others fled. His love
would not let him be wholly separated from Christ,
and love on this night, as at all times, covers a multitude of sins. But it has a bad side also, in that Peter,
after his proud boastings and declarations of loyalty
and his readiness to go to prison and to death, now
takes a safe position far in the rear. "Peter followed afar off."

In this respect, Peter is a type of many Chris-

tians who follow their Lord, but afar off. Some
do this, as Peter did, through fear; not the fear
now of what Peter dreaded, prison, violence, and
death—although that may come again in the history of the Church, and Christians again be driven
to the Catacombs—but the fear of the world's scorn
or laughter or mockery. But when it comes to a
choice between the smile of Christ and the laughter
or the frown of this world, the soul ought not to
hesitate.

Some, again, follow Christ afar off because they
are caught in the stream of the world. There is no
hostility to Christ, or to his Church. There are no
troubling doubts concerning the great doctrines or
truths, yet they follow afar off. Only occasionally
are they seen at worship or at prayer. Isaiah ridiculed the idolater who went out into the forest to
cut down a tree out of which to make an idol, but
used most of the tree for firewood to warm himself
and to cook his food, and of the residue made his
god. There are many whose religion is a residue,
or left-over religion. These persons may be well-
wishers of Christ. They may have some true yearn-
ings for the religious life, but because they follow
afar off they do not count on the side of Christ. His
foes, so far as they are concerned, can do to Christ
what they please. "He that is not with me is against
me; and he that gathereth not with me scattereth
abroad."

There are those who follow Christ afar off because they have been caught in the whirl of that world which is spoken of as "society." Their names appear often in the society and smart set columns of the paper, and at social affairs in the interests of charity; but they do not appear in the columns of the Church, of those who work for Christ. In their life there flows, no doubt, a sub-surface stream of religious desire; but it is given only an occasional expression in public worship, or in active Christian witness. Their time, energy, talent, training, heredity are devoted to that which, in the end, profiteth nothing. How often I have looked upon people like this who are associated with the Church, and have said to myself, "What a friend of Christ you could be, and what a strength to his Church, if you would only give your time and energy and enthusiasm to that which is of the highest value." It is to them, more than to any others, that the words of the prophet apply: "Wherefore do ye spend money for that which is not bread, and your labor for that which satisfieth not?"

She was a woman who even in the decline of old age showed vestiges of a remarkable early beauty. Daughter of a governor of one of the Eastern States, she had been a great belle in her youth, and her beauty had even led a distracted suitor to shoot another. Well do I remember what she said to me one day when some reference was made to the world of society which she had abandoned completely for the Church, its services, its friendships, and its sacred causes. "I've been all through that. There's nothing in it."

There are others, again, who follow afar off, because of something not right in their lives, and that something keeps them in the rear. What could be sadder than the state of one who owns the beauty and the power of the Christian life, will not cut himself off altogether from the Church or from prayer, yet will not break with some evil habit, or unwholesome companionship, or secret sin which holds him far in the rear?

Peter followed afar off. The danger of such a relationship with Christ is illustrated in the history of Peter on this night. First there was compromise and disguise. Peter sat down among the foes of Christ and talked with them as if he were one of them, instead of a disciple of Christ. Then came the temptation, the sad denial, and the fall. "And Peter went out and wept bitterly." He had done what he thought he could never do, because he had followed afar off.

When we follow Christ afar off we miss the joy and peace of the Christian life. That was a sad night for Peter. Even before he actually cursed his Lord and denied him, he must have been wretchedly unhappy; and when he swore and cursed, he was swearing more at himself than at any other. If you are following Christ as Peter did that night, afar off, then close up the gap and draw nigh to God. Christ invites us to the closest relationship. He calls us friends. "Behold, I stand at the door, and knock: if any man hear my voice, and open the door, I will come in to him, and will sup with him, and he with me."

> "Come, lest the heart should, cold and cast away,
>     Die ere the Guest adored she entertain;
>   Lest eyes which never saw Thine early day
>     Should miss Thy heavenly reign."

Peter followed afar off that night. Yet the last word of Jesus to Peter was what he said to him that morning by the Sea of Galilee, and what he says to us today, even those who have followed the farthest off, or have denied him as Peter did, "Follow thou me."

## PETER'S TEARS

## IX

*"And Peter went out, and wept bitterly"*

Luke 22: 62

BUT a moment ago this man was saying before all the disciples that he would follow his Master to prison and to death, and even if he had to die with Christ, he would not deny him. A moment ago his sword was flashing in the moonlight of Gethsemane as he struck at one of those who came to attack his Master. Now we behold a broken man going quickly out into the night and weeping bitterly. Not since our first parents wept at the gates of lost Eden, had such bitter tears been shed. Men have wept for joy when they found that which was lost or were restored to lost friends. Men have wept when death put the seal of eternal silence upon lips of those they loved to hear speaking. Men have wept over the pains of their own body, or when for one another's woes there has flowed the sympathizing tear. But the bitterest tears are the tears of Peter. The tears do not always run down the cheek nor are the sobs always heard by man. Sometimes they are the tears that flow within the heart and the sobs that echo in the solitary places of the soul. They are the tears that are shed over the saddest sin in the world, the sin of treason to the soul.

All sin is sad. I wonder if sadness is not the best description of God's attitude toward sin. We speak of the wrath of God, but it is the wrath of infinite sorrow, for the heart of the Eternal is most wonderfully kind. Suppose that a kind and worthy father has a son, and that son falls into sin, perhaps into actual crime. We put ourselves in that father's place and at once our chief feeling is one of sorrow. When David heard that the profligate Absalom had fallen in battle, it was with sorrow that he thought of the wayward son, now gone to his reckoning. How the words of that father echo and re-echo through the aisles of time, finding a response in every disappointed father's heart: "O my son Absalom, my son, my son Absalom! would God I had died for thee, O Absalom, my son, my son!" There is, indeed, a truth in those presentations of the atonement which lay the emphasis upon the wrath of God toward sin as exemplified in the death of Christ on the Cross. But we must never forget to make mention too of the sorrow of God, the yearning love that was back of the whole transaction, "for God so loved the world, that he gave his only begotten Son, that whosoever believeth in him might not perish, but have everlasting life." The pathos of sin is expressed in what God has done to redeem man out of his sins. Any state in man that required the supreme tragedy of the Cross must be sad, infinitely sad.

I do not know that anywhere else, in the Bible or out of it, is there a verse or a phrase which so creates in our minds a feeling of the sadness of sin as this phrase which comes at the end of the recital of Peter's doings on that eventful night, "He went out, and wept bitterly." We are not angry with Peter as we are with Judas, the deliberate traitor; nor greatly amazed at this deed. Our first and last feeling is one of sadness. We could almost weep with him. There are writers who make you weep as they recite the wrongs and sufferings of mankind; and others who can make you weep with the lover or maid upon whom the tragedy of life has fallen; and others, like Charles Dickens, who can make you weep over the deathbed of innocence and beauty, "Little Paul" and "Little Nell." But the Bible makes you weep over sin. For true pathos this scene is incomparable. And these writers, who were they? Professional men of letters, making it their business to stir the deep places of human nature? No; the ancient writers hardly knew what the sentiments of compassion and tenderness were; it was Christianity that introduced them into the world. These writers were just four plain men, only one of them, Luke, perhaps, of any education; yet they have told the story, each in his own way, that is the world's masterpiece of pathos.

## I. THE SIN OF DISLOYALTY TO SELF

We follow the other dark actor in this tragedy of the last night of our Lord's life until he goes out into the night and hangs himself. The deeds and the suicide of Judas alarm us and amaze us, and his violent self-inflicted death shocks us. We feel that we have been witnessing a dark tragedy of human nature; but that feeling of sadness that comes over us when we hear Peter curse his Master, and then go out into the night and weep bitterly, is totally wanting in the case of Judas. What is the difference? It is the difference of intention and purpose. Judas did what he wanted to do, what he planned to do, what he was paid to do; but Peter did what he had not planned to do, what he had not wished to do, what he had been warned against doing, what he declared he could never do. The despair of Judas is the despair of a man who finds that, instead of gaining by his evil deed, he has lost, and lost heavily, lost all that he has. But the tears of Peter are the tears of a man who suddenly awakens to the fact that he has done the very thing he hated, and left undone the thing he wanted to do. That is the saddest sin in the world, not the sin of the hardened wretch who carries out his long-conceived iniquity, but the sin of the man who purposes good in his heart and is suddenly and completely overcome with temptation.

[ 95 ]

In the larger sense, Peter was disloyal to himself. There were two Peters—the Peter of the impulsive affection and ringing declaration of loyalty, the Peter of the flashing sword, and the Peter of the denying oaths. It was because he realized that he had a better self, that he had wished to be true and loyal to Christ, that he wept such bitter tears over his complete failure. Back of all the mistakes and blunders and faults of man, there flows that fountain of sorrow. That drunkard lying in the doorway of the closed shop at evening, as the people hurry to their homes; at first you think of him as a fool, but who knows what sorrow will be in his heart when he comes again to himself? Who knows that he did not set out that day with far different thoughts in his heart and far different purposes than to lie for the sport or passing sigh of the multitude until the patrol wagon took him to the station? Who knows that he had not set out to purchase Christmas gifts for his wife and his children? When you look upon him, think of Peter's tears. Those prisoners that we see getting out of the wagons at the City Hall, and whom we are disposed to regard as belonging, as some of them do, to the professional criminal set, perhaps far more of them than we imagine commenced the day, that ends so darkly for them, with far other thoughts in their hearts than to do the deeds that have brought them into prison. They may have commenced the day with purposes as honorable as dwelt in your heart when you arose on this day of rest and worship. But the tempter met them where they least expected to encounter him; the accidents or the incidents of the day roused anger or passion or greed. When you think of the penitentiary, with its long corridors and hundreds of men clad in fustian, think of them as not all Judases to right and good. Think of the Peters among them; not all deliberate sinners and criminals, but victims of surprise on the part of that worse and dangerous self who lurks in your breast and in mine.

But to illustrate my thesis it is not necessary that we should confine ourselves to the instances of gross transgression. After all, Peter's sin was not a sin of the hand or the eye or the tongue, but a sin of the heart. If there are none who can honestly say that they have been absolutely faithful to their best selves, how many there must be who have to plead guilty to having frequently fallen far short of that standard which they had set before them, of having been openly disloyal to that better self they had pledged themselves to follow. If we are thoughtful at all, we must be often saddened by the recollection of how easily laziness and cowardice and worldliness have allured us from the path of that duty that we had commenced to follow. You took stock of yourself and found that there were many things in your life that you ought to change. But have you changed them? Are you changing them? Are you really try-

ing to change them? Look back tonight over this
year fast drawing to a close: Has it been the improve-
ment upon previous years that it ought to have
been, that it might have been? You realize that there
were certain mistakes that you had made in the past
and determined that you would not make them in the
future. How is it with you tonight? Have you repeated them? Has the morning of promise ended in
the night of disappointment and failure? There were
certain unfortunate habits of disposition or of action, and you resolved to break them. Have they
been broken, or has another year only made them all
the harder to break? There were sins that did so
easily beset you in the past. You resolved, it may
be in solemn reverent earnest prayer, that you would
lay them aside. Have you done that? Or do they
find it easier and easier to beset you and overcome
you? And if we must confess, so many of us, to
this charge of infidelity to that higher self within
us, can that be anything but sad? Are we different
from Peter, in kind, or only in degree? His failure was complete, a complete repudiation of the
higher self on the part of the lower. But our failure, though perhaps not so tragic nor so striking, is
of a kind. Matthew and Luke end this account of
Peter by saying that "he went out and wept bitterly."
But Mark's account has a word of suggestion in it,
"When he thought thereon, he wept." When he
thought thereon! When you think "Thereon"—

on yourself, on your present and your past and your opportunities, on your purposes and advantages and examples and blessings and warnings and prayers, your own and those of others—is it altogether joy and exaltation? or does an element of sadness creep over your meditation and self-examination?

> "As some most pure and noble face,
>   Seen in the thronged and hurrying street,
>   Sheds o'er the world a sudden grace,
>   A flying odour sweet—
>   Then, passing, leaves the cheated sense
>   Balked with a phantom excellence:
>   So, on our souls the visions rise
>   Of that fair life we never led:
>   They flash a splendor past our eyes,
>   We start, and they are fled:
>   They pass, and leave us with blank gaze,
>   Resigned to our ignoble days." [1]

## II. Infidelity to Christ

I have been speaking of moral action in general terms and the sorrow which goes with failure and inconstancy. But more definitely, let us turn to the immediate circumstances of the sin of Peter and speak of the Christian's disloyalty to Christ. I do not speak now of his scorners and contemners, open and arrogant foes, but of his friends. Here was a

[1] William Watson. John Lane Company.

man who set out to follow Christ that day: See where he ended. In his hour of crisis he failed dismally and completely. That always hurts: not that we have failed to do all that we ought to have done in our ordinary commonplace hours of life, but that when the great crisis arose, calling for unfaltering and unflinching courage, we have not been able to meet the test. How often do the disciples of Jesus repeat the sin of Peter! No loud oaths are spoken, no hostile guards or servants stand about us; but suddenly there strikes the hour for us to witness to our discipleship by a splendid loyalty and ringing testimony, that which we do or refuse to do, what we say, or what we refuse to say, what we give or what we withdraw; and when the hour has passed we know that we have failed, failed ourselves, failed the Saviour. We feel like those sleeping disciples in Gethsemane when Jesus came and found them sleeping, and rousing them said to them, "What! could ye not watch with me one hour?" One hour!

Peter had been solemnly warned by Jesus, who told him that Satan desired to have him that he might sift him as wheat. He had warned himself. So far as we can see he took every precaution. He had followed cautiously afar off, and when he finally appeared at the fireside to "see the end of the thing," humanly speaking, he was armed on every side. And yet, when the sudden accusation of the servant girl was brought against him, giving him one of the greatest opportunities that Christian disciple ever had to confess Jesus before the world, Peter failed.

It is common to talk of Peter as being an impulsive, mercurial nature, the winds of his enthusiasm quickly rising and as quickly subsiding. But the more I think about him, the less I think of this explanation of his character. He failed where so many others fail, and as a miniature gathers into the little space all the characteristics of the subject's face and expression, so looking this night into the face of Peter, I see a miniature of Christian experience. Perhaps the motive of fear was uppermost in Peter's mind when he denied Christ, but the particular motive makes little difference. How often we repeat the sin of Peter! Our judgment now declares itself on the side of Christ; our hearts go out to him in loving adoration; we admire the sweet majesty of his Person; but before this week is over, you, and you, and you, will have denied Christ. Suppose that he were to be present when you act; within hearing always when you speak, within sight when you move, outwardly, before men, or in the solitudes of the soul. How often he would be grieved! How oft surprised! How oft he would turn and look in hurt amazement to see if this is really that disciple of his who sang so earnestly the hymns and bowed so reverently before him in the House of Prayer. I am not referring to disciples who are insincere—you could not bring such a charge against Peter—but to those who are sincere, who truly desire to be faithful to Christ and to confess him before men. This was the sorrow of a man who had vowed, who had prayed, who had tried, who had listened to Christ, who had followed him; yet he failed.

If, then, on the part of such disciples the experience of Peter will be repeated from day to day, what are we to infer about the Christian life? Just two things, one negative and the other positive: First, that in human nature there is a stubborn hostility to Christ and all that is of Christ. No one naturally lives the Christian life, and now and then men and women upon whom we look as leaning even in their failures to the side of Christ and virtue, surprise the world with an inner history of constant struggle and prayer. The moment the heart declares for Christ, there is war within. The law of sin begins at that moment its assault upon the law of Christ. The second thing that I infer from the experience of a good man like Peter, and the multitudes of Christians who have come after him, each in his turn going out into the night to weep, is that, not only is there in my nature that which is hostile to Christ and makes war upon my better self which declares for Christ, but that, so far as my own strength and skill are concerned, that worst anti-Christian self will get the victory. When it comes to a clash of arms he is usually the strongest. I do my best, and then fail, and like Paul I cry out, "O wretched man that I am! who shall deliver me?" I do my best and then fail like Peter, and can only mourn over my failure.

Alas! of myself I can do nothing. The battle is lost before I commence it. What then shall I do? My hope is in the experience of Peter, just as my danger is in the experience of Peter. And what happened to Peter? How does it come that this fisherman, so cowardly, so cringing, his cruel oaths sounding in the ears of Jesus and hurting more than the fists of the mob or the blows of the soldiers, appears after a little as the mighty apostle, strengthening all who are persecuted and afraid by his lionlike boldness and unfaltering faith and courage? We can account for that transformation upon just one ground: It was hinted at by our Lord when he warned Peter against his fall: "When thou art converted, strengthen thy brethren." Peter had not yet been converted; he had not yet turned his heart to Christ. When that took place, it is a new and victorious man that we see in the glorious dawn of Christianity. His experience is our hope. We must ask God to convert us wholly to his will. There is a tendency in the Church today to look upon the Christian life as a life that man can live by himself. He cannot; it is the life that he lives in Christ. A Christian man is a miracle, the perennial miracle of the grace of God. To realize that is really the first step in the Christian life. Outside of Christ you will fail. You may measure up the world's thought or idea of a Christian; but until you have been converted, turned by the Spirit of God, you cannot do, you cannot be, what God would have you to be.

It is possible that what I have been saying about the saddest sin in the world has been of a nature to depress and discourage some of you. You compare what you are and what you have been with what you desire to be and what you planned to do, and must confess that in many ways you have failed, and that as a man you have failed; as a Christian you have denied him. Why should I remind you of what cannot now be helped? Because it is that very sense of failure, that very feeling of sadness that comes over us, that is our hope for the future. Peter wept bitterly and it was the tears of Peter that saved him. He feared that his sin was fatal, that his loss was irrevocable, and so long as he was ready to weep over such a calamity befalling him, there was hope for him. That was the first step toward his conversion. He was cleansed by his tears. In the dark night his grief became his star of hope. If you have followed him in his denial, follow him out into the night of sorrow and repentance, and you too will know the joys of salvation; you will begin to see that Christ in you is greater than he that is in the world, and that he is able to keep you from falling and to present you faultless before the presence of his Glory.

# PETER AT THE TOMB

## X

### John 20: 1-9

LAST week we left Peter out in the night. And what a night it was for him, weeping those bitter tears of shame, and remorse, and sorrow, the bitterest tears that have been shed since our first parents wept at the gates of the Lost Eden. But in that night there were two stars for Peter: one was the look, that marvelous look, that look of pain and grief; but also of love and pity and yearning which Christ had turned upon Peter when he heard his coarse and brutal denial. This was a look from Jesus, but there is nothing in the Bible which presents more clearly or more beautifully the work of the Holy Spirit. It is the mission of the Holy Spirit to work repentance and faith in the sinner's heart, to show him his sin and point him to the mercy of God. That was what the look of Christ did for Peter on that dark night; "when he thought thereon, he wept." Peter out in the night remembered that look. How can he ever forget it! The other star on this black night was Peter's recollection of the prayer that Christ made for him at the Supper, that his faith might not fail; and with that prayer went the definite promise that it would not fail, and that Peter was to have a part in the ministry of Christ. "When thou art converted, strengthen thy brethren." In the darkness of that bitter hour, Peter, we may be sure, remembers these things.

The veil of silence now falls over Peter until the morning of the Resurrection. It is pure conjecture, of course, and imagination; but I like to think that John, who must have heard Peter's denial and saw him when he went out weeping bitterly, followed him out into the night and did what he could to console him and strengthen him. So far as we know, none of the disciples was present at the trial before Pilate. You can imagine Peter, wherever he was, waiting in the deepest distress for news about Jesus; and when he heard that he was condemned his heart must have smitten him afresh when he remembered his denial. When Christ was led out to Calvary, who knows that Peter with anguish in his heart saw his Lord as he passed through the streets, or fell beneath his too heavy Cross.

John was probably the only disciple present at the Crucifixion; at least, there is no mention of any other. But the mother of Jesus was there with the sword piercing her heart, as the aged Simeon had predicted when he held the child in his arms in the temple. "Yea, a sword shall pierce through thine own soul also." The two thieves were there also: the one cursing and reviling, and the other lamenting. The Scribes and the Pharisees were there to mock him; and the women that had followed him from Galilee were there, standing afar off and beholding. When the last cry, "It is finished!" had broken from the lips of Christ, and the veil in the temple had been rent in twain and the graves opened, it was not the disciples of Jesus who did him the last sad office and took his body down from the Cross, but two others, Joseph of Arimathea and the secret night disciple, who now comes gloriously out into the daylight of open and courageous testimony, Nicodemus. The women followed the body of Christ to the grave and saw where they had laid him. Apparently, they were the last to leave the sepulcher on Friday night. When Saturday, or the Sabbath, was over, early in the morning of the first day of the week, they went out with spices and ointments to anoint the body of Jesus. They were saying among themselves, "Who shall roll us away the stone from the door of the tomb?" when to their amazement they saw that the stone was already rolled back. One of the women, and who apparently did not wait to hear what the angels told the other women, was Mary of Magdala. Distressed at seeing the grave of Christ empty, she ran back to the city and exclaimed to Peter and John, "They have taken away the Lord out of the tomb, and we know not where they have laid him."

Everything in the beautiful narrative here points to the fact that Peter is at the house of John, if John had a home in Jerusalem. Evidently he had, for "from that hour" he took the mother of Jesus into his own home. This would seem to tell us that John has taken Peter into his own home, and that he is doing what he can to comfort him and restore him. If so, it is a beautiful commentary on John's friendship for Peter. A single unworthy act, base, indeed, though that was, John would not permit to wreck and destroy the friendship of years with Peter. When they heard the tidings, it was Peter who first of all acted. "Peter," John writes, "therefore went forth, and that other disciple, and came to the sepulcher." Whenever anything is to be done, it is Peter who takes the lead. He is the first to speak and the first to act. John followed him, and together they ran to the sepulcher. Just how much more was in their mind than that the grave of Christ had been profaned, and his body stolen, we do not know. Perhaps there was stirring in their heart the thought, at least the hope, that Christ was alive. On the race of the tomb, the other disciple John did outrun Peter, and came first to the sepulcher. Probably John was younger and more agile than Peter, and that was the reason he outran him. It certainly was not because he was more eager to get to the sepulcher than Peter. Coming first to the tomb, and stooping down and looking into it, John saw enough to let him know that it surely was empty, for he saw at a glance the linen clothes lying on the pavement. But John went no further than the mouth of the sepulcher. What held him back? Was it a natural awe and wonder at what might be a resurrection, or was it the Hebrew dread of profanation and defilement at the place of the dead, or was it just a natural fear, for no one likes to go into a grave? But while John stands hesitating, Peter comes panting up, and without a moment's delay goes down into the sepulcher and, looking about, sees the linen clothes lying on the stones, and also, and very important, what John had not seen, the napkin that had been about the head of Christ lying in a place by itself. This must have suggested to Peter that there had been no hasty exit or hurried stealing of a body, but something deliberate, calm, and majestic. When John saw that Peter had suffered no harm, or perhaps when he had heard a call from Peter, he himself went down to the sepulcher, and he saw and believed. This, John records, was the way he and Peter came to believe that Christ was risen, for, he adds, "they knew not the scripture that he must rise again from the dead." Strange, indeed, that they did not remember what Jesus had said about his resurrection. The only ones who seemed to remember it were the Scribes and Pharisees, who, when they asked Pilate for a guard at the grave, recalled Jesus' prediction of a resurrection, saying, "Sir, we remember that

that deceiver said, while he was yet alive, After three days I will rise again."

Horace Bushnell has a famous sermon on this text: "Then entered in also that other disciple, which came first to the sepulcher, and he saw, and believed." What he draws from this fact is the impressive lesson of our unconscious influence. John stopped, hesitating at the mouth of the sepulcher. Peter, when he came up second in the race, went boldly in and saw the evidences of a resurrection. He was not consciously influencing John; nevertheless what he did gave John the courage to follow his example, and going into the tomb, John saw and believed.

Every Christian ought to be exerting a deliberate and conscious influence upon others for good. The great disease of the Church is the lack of that effort. Christ says to all of us, "Ye shall be my witnesses" —witnesses unto me. Every Christian can make some sort of a witness for Christ. Some of the least can do the most. Frequently in the Scriptures, great events are brought to pass by humble actors. The servant of Saul, when Saul wanted to turn back, brings him into the presence of Samuel and face to face with his destiny. The servant of Naaman, when that satrap was in a rage at Elisha, reminded him that he had come to Samaria to be cured of his leprosy and persuaded him to use the cure that Elisha had prescribed. It was a captive maid in Naaman's house who had told him of the prophet of God. Humble agents can help to work great destinies. Let none, therefore, hold back because he thinks he is not gifted, or that his post is not important enough. Who can tell the effect and influence of an earnest word to another in the interests of his highest happiness and the welfare of his soul—a word of comfort, a word of hope, or a word of warning; a word spoken in season, how good it is? The author of that Proverb does not say, "a word spoken in season" by a learned man, or an eloquent man, or a clever man, or a great man, but a word spoken in season, how good it is. "In the morning sow thy seed, and in the evening withhold not thine hand." "Cast thy bread upon the waters: for thou shalt find it after many days."

But the influence that Peter exerted upon John here was an indirect and unconscious influence. Peter was acting for himself, but he was acting courageously and earnestly, and it had its result, its influence, upon another life. We shall speak more of this when we come to the story of Peter's shadow, how when he went down the streets of Jerusalem he healed with his shadow those who could not get within the reach of his touch. We all have our shadow lives. There is a spontaneous going forth of influence, and whether it is a good or bad influence depends upon the state of the heart. If we would influence others for good, then let us live near to Christ ourselves. John the Baptist is spoken of as a burning and a shining light. He shone because he burned. Where we burn with the true love for Christ, there we shall send forth a helpful and, it may be, a saving light.

Stephen Grellet, the noted Friend, once in this country felt a burden on his heart and the leading of the Holy Spirit to preach the gospel to men in a lumber camp. But when he arrived at the camp he found it deserted, for the men had gone farther into the forest. But feeling that he had been sent there by the Holy Spirit, he stood up in the empty mess hall and delivered his sermon, as he thought, heard only by the board walls of the building and the lofty trees of the forest. Years afterward, crossing London Bridge in the evening gloom, he was somewhat rudely stopped by a man who accosted him and said: "You are the man I have been looking for all these years. I have found you at last." "But," said Grellet, surprised, "there must be some mistake. I have never seen thee." "No," said the man. "Did you not preach at a lumber camp in the American forest?" "Yes," said Grellet, "but there was no one there." "But I was there," said the man, "and I heard the sermon." Then he went on to relate how he had come back from where the men were working to get a saw that had been left behind, when he was startled and alarmed at hearing the sound of a man's voice. Approaching the building he looked through a chink of the logs and saw Grellet standing by himself preaching the sermon. He listened to the preacher, was convicted of sin, got hold of a copy of the Scriptures, learned the way of life, was saved, and brought others with him into the Kingdom of Heaven.

I imagine there will be some great surprises in that other world. Indeed, Christ says that it will be so, for he pictures those who have been faithful and merciful in this life saying in surprise to Jesus, "But when saw we thee athirst, or a hungered, or sick, or in prison?" Yes, there will be great surprises in that heavenly life. Let us so live that we shall reap some of those pleasant surprises. What could be worse than to reap unpleasant surprises, and to learn how our word, or example, or deed, influenced others for evil and not for good? But what could be better, what more joyful, than to reap pleasant surprises, to hear men and women, redeemed souls, say, "Your word, your character, your example, your faith, helped me and strengthened me. Had it not been for you, I might not be here today."

## PETER RESTORED

### XI

## *"Feed my sheep"*

John 21: 17

THERE were three steps in the restoration of the fallen Peter. The first was the message which the two angels gave to the women at the tomb. "He is risen; he is not here: behold the place where they laid him. But go, tell his disciples *and Peter*." What a wealth of meaning is poured into that phrase *"and Peter"*! It was the angels' message to Peter, and what a message of grace and forgiveness it was! The women might well have thought that the one who had denied that he had ever seen or known Jesus could not now be included in the number of the disciples. Lest, therefore, in their message they should pass by Peter, the angels make it clear that Peter also is to be told of the resurrection of Jesus, and directed to the place where he might meet him. So the angels of God's mercy bring sweet messages to our spirits, even when we have denied our Lord and sinned against him. *"And Peter."* That means that Christ does not forget his disciples even when they forget him. He sends a special messenger and message to woo us back to his loving heart.

The inference from St. Luke's account of the first Sunday evening is that Christ had appeared to Peter alone of all the disciples, for when the two to whom Christ had disclosed himself on the way to Emmaus returned to Jerusalem, where the eleven were gathered together, they heard from their lips, "The Lord is risen indeed, and hath appeared to Simon." In his catalogue of the appearances of Christ after his resurrection, St. Paul lists this appearance to Peter first. "He appeared to Cephas, then to the twelve." Of all the appearances, this is the one about which we would like to know the most. But something has sealed the lips of the evangelist, and even of St. Paul; for, other than the fact, we are told nothing about this appearance. Perhaps it was too sacred even for the records of the gospel.

The next step in the restoration of Peter was our Lord's conversation with him on that memorable morning on the shore of the Sea of Galilee. This great picture is painted for us by the one who was best qualified to do it, that disciple whom Jesus loved, St. John. This, I think, is perhaps the most wonderful scene in the New Testament.

If one wants evidence for the truth and inspiration of the Gospels, one need not go further afield than to read this last chapter of John's Gospel, in which he relates the meeting between Peter and his Lord.

The last time we saw Peter was at night, when, having denied his Lord, he went out and wept bitterly. But now it is morning, and a double morning it was for Peter. Seven of the disciples have gone down to the Sea of Galilee to resume their old trade as fishermen. Of these seven, five are named—Peter, Thomas, Nathanael, the sons of Zebedee, James and John; and two others are unnamed. We cannot help wondering where the other five were, or, rather, the other four, for we know where Judas was. All through the night the disciples have been dragging their nets, and perhaps now and then reminding one another of how on that same sea Christ had called them to be fishers of men. The morning has come and they have taken nothing. The mists are lifting from the surface of the sea as the light begins to break over the eastern mountains. In the uncertain light of the early morning, as they are dragging in the empty nets to the deck of the gently swaying fishing boat, they discern the figure of a solitary man standing on the shore. He calls to them, "Children, have ye any meat?" When they answer "No," he tells them to cast the net on the right side of the ship. By this time John is sure that it is Jesus, and he says to Peter, "It is the Lord!" The moment he heard that, Peter did just what you would have expected him to do: he leaped into the sea and swam and waded the one hundred yards between him and the shore. The other disciples followed him, and soon they were all seated about the fire on which was fish and bread. It was probably a silent meal, for, as John puts it in his quaint style, "None of them durst ask him, Who art thou? knowing that it was the Lord." No doubt, too, the other six were wondering what Jesus would have to say to Peter. If so, they soon learned.

When the meal was over, Jesus turned to Peter and said—what?—"How could you have denied me?" —"Do you still think yourself worthy to be with the disciples?"—"What is the difference between your sin and the sin of Judas?" No, not that, not a single reference to the past, or the dark tragedy of Peter's denial; but this: "Lovest thou me?" When Peter had been given an opportunity to confess his love three times, as he had thrice denied Jesus, then Jesus said to him, "Feed my sheep." The past was blotted out; its dark sin was forgiven and forgotten. Peter is restored to his place as an apostle, and is given another chance.

Few books get so far back into the hidden places of the soul and reveal its abysmal capacity for suffering as the Autobiography of Mark Rutherford. In one of those gripping pages he relates how he was delivered out of the depths of despair and self-accusation by the kindness of a friend. He concludes his account of the incident with this sentence: "I should like to add one more beatitude to those of the Gospels, and to say, 'Blessed are they who heal us of self-despisings.' Of all services which can be done to man I know of none more precious." The most exquisite illustration of this beatitude is found in the history of Peter. Peter had wounded the One whom he loved, and this always produces the sharpest pain and the deepest remorse. It is one thing to heal a man of despising others, or hating others or wronging others; but to heal a man of self-despising, that is the most difficult and delicate cure of all.

When he saw Christ on that morning through the lifting mists, the recollection of what he had done to him must have come back to Peter like the stab of a knife. But now he is told that all that past is forgotten and blotted out. He is to commence a new race and start another chapter. Not only is his sin forgiven, but he is granted a great commission and sent forth on a great mission to preach the gospel and feed the sheep of Christ. If Christ had said to Thomas, who had expressed some melancholy doubts, and was reluctant to believe in the Resurrection, but yet had never denied his Lord, "Feed my sheep," or if he had said it to Matthew or to John, or to Philip, or any of the other six who sat about the fire on that spring morning on the shore of the Sea of Galilee, "Feed my sheep," it would not have been strange. The strange thing, the glorious thing, and, for you and me, the encouraging thing, is that

[ 118 ]

he said it to Peter, the disciple who with an oath had denied that he ever knew him. Someone has expressed the thought—

"I wish that there were some wonderful place
    Called the Land of Beginning Again,
Where all our mistakes and all our heartaches
    And all of our poor selfish grief
Could be dropped like a shabby old coat at the door,
    And never put on again.

I wish we could come on it all unaware,
    Like the hunter who finds a lost trail;
I wish that the one who our blindness has done
    The greatest injustice of all
Could be at the gates, like an old friend who waits
    For the comrade he's gladdest to hail." [1]

This is a song which from time to time has an echo, sometimes faint, sometimes strong in our own hearts. What with us may seem to be a very real, but almost impossible, wish, in Christ is the great reality. Christianity is a highway that leads to the Land of Beginning Again. How often that word "new" occurs in the Scriptures and in Christian theology: the *new* Testament or *new* Covenant, the *new* creature, the *new* man, the *new* birth, the *new* commandment, the *new* name, the *new* song, and the *new* heaven and *new* earth.

[1] Louisa Tarkington.

The first Sunday of a new year has a moral value because it brings men to think of things that they will not wish to carry over into the new year. As we turn over the leaves of the calendar of the past, we come now and then upon a blank page, or a blotted page, or a torn page, and other pages which, because they bear the record of transgression or weakness or failure or omission, we would just as soon pass over. No doubt, there are some who are a little heavy-hearted as they look back and see how last year they did just about the same as the year before, repeating its blunders and mistakes, and therefore hardly expecting that the year to come will tell the story of a better record. But it *ought* to be better. It *can* be better. There is none here today for whom it *ought not* to be better, and none for whom it *cannot* be better.

We may be able to see and understand how the struggles, or hardships, or trials of our life have been for our good, refining our spirits, disciplining our minds, and teaching us to love that which has lasting worth. When we have passed through these things we can sometimes say with the Psalmist, "It was for my good that I was afflicted." Even if we cannot affirm it at the time, yet afterwards, and looking backwards, we can say, "It was for my good."

But what shall we say of the moral failures, the transgressions, and the sins of the past? Into what scheme of compensation or spiritual profit and recompense can we fit these things? The first cloud of evil that traversed the bright sky of youth's innocence; the strange, alarming silence of the first guilt; the half lies which were spoken in quick self-defense; the careless injury to another's name; or the positive seeking out of evil, or the hidden transgression—how strange is the vitality of these things! The old mythology told of a river down which men floated, looking with delight upon flowery banks and green shores and blue skies, until suddenly by their side in the river they found themselves looking into the features of fear and guilt and accusation.

Memory is like that river. Now it opens for us a charming landscape, bright sunshine, green meadows, gracious shade trees, and all manner of wild flowers; and then quickly changes and carries us under leaden skies and through a bleak and barren country. A book, a date, a picture, a face; and that's enough to blot out the sun! When Christ died on the Cross we read that the graves were opened. Figuratively speaking, that is what happens in a great many cases when the true gospel is preached. The graves are opened! Why do some men not go to Church? Because they regard what is proclaimed as myth or legend? Not always. Because the preaching is stupid and dull? Not always. Because the music is raucous? Not always. There is another reason: Because when they come *the graves are opened!*

Human wisdom has no system or plan for dealing

with the mistakes of yesterday. All that it can do is to hand us over to the assaults of conscience or, when conscience is seared, to dreary deadness and dullness. But what is not possible with man is possible with God. God fits the past into His grand plan of repentance and faith. What the law could not do, God, sending his Son in the likeness of sinful flesh to die for man, has done.

Here we find the enthusiasm, the hope, and the joy of our Christian faith. In the mystery of his cross, God neutralizes the effects of sin, forgives its offense, blots out its stain, expiates its guilt, and offers a new chance. This was what he did for Peter when he said to him, "Feed my sheep." Henceforth, the apostle of weakness and denial becomes the apostle of heroic faith and boldness. We might have had a Peter who never fell and never was restored. But such a Peter, however worthy and admirable, would never have come as close to us as the Peter of these two great scenes—midnight in the High Priest's court, sunrise on the Sea of Galilee.

Every day opens a door of repentance and opportunity. The Land of Beginning Again has no barriers, no customs, and no examinations. The only passport it requires is sincerity of purpose. There is a legend that Peter, when he was preaching, would sometimes hear the crow of a nearby cock. At first he would hesitate and falter for a moment, and then resume his preaching with greater power and zeal

than before. By the grace of God even the marred
and broken past becomes our strength. Men have
spoken of some liquid or acid which, when poured
on ashes, would transmute the ashes to purest gold.
What is chemically impossible and inconceivable, is
possible, and not only possible, but, as in the case of
Peter, and many a sinner since, actual and historic.
A man who once applied for a position with a manufacturer began to refer with apology to some unhappy incident in his past. The manufacturer said,
"I don't care about the past. Start where you
stand."

"Start where you stand and never mind the past,
    The past won't help you in beginning new.
If you are done with it at last,
    Why, that's enough. You're done with it, you're
        through;
This is another chapter in the book,
    This is another race that you have planned.
Don't give the vanished days a backward look,
    Start where you stand.

The world won't care about your old defeats.
    If you can start anew and win success,
The future is your time, and time is fleet,
    And there is much of work and strain and stress;
Forget the buried woes and dead despairs.
    Here is a brand-new trial right at hand,
The future is for him who does and dares—
    Start where you stand.

Old failures will not halt, old triumphs aid;
　Today's the thing, tomorrow soon will be;
Get in the fight and face it, unafraid,
　And leave the past to ancient history;
What has been, has been; yesterday is dead,
　And by it you are neither blessed nor banned;
Take courage, man, be brave and drive ahead—
　Start where you stand!" [2]

# PETER AND TOMORROW

## XII

### *"Follow thou me"*

John 21: 22

THE close relationship between Peter and John is one of the interesting and beautiful associations of the New Testament. They were partners as fishermen on the Sea of Galilee, and both had become disciples of John the Baptist before they were called by Christ. Together with James, they formed an elect company whom Jesus took with him when he raised the dead, and up to the Mount of Transfiguration, and who were asked to watch with him in his agony at Gethsemane. At the Supper, Peter whispered to John to ask Jesus who the traitor was. On the night of the betrayal, John spoke to Peter and had him admitted to the court-yard of the high priest. On the day of the Resurrection the two men together ran to the sepulcher, John, evidently the younger, outrunning Peter. In the Book of the Acts we find them in prison together and bearing witness to the risen Christ.

One of the most interesting of these contacts of

Peter with John is related by John in the last chapter
of his Gospel. That chapter is one of the beautiful
masterpieces of the Bible. When Christ, walking
along the shore of the Sea of Galilee in the early
morning, hailed the fishermen apostles and asked
them if they had any meat, and then told them to
cast the net on the right side of the ship, it was John,
far-discerning John, who said to Peter, "It is the
Lord." After they had dined with Christ on the
shore, Jesus gave Peter an opportunity thrice to
avow his love as he had thrice denied him. Then he
said to him, "Feed my sheep." This was followed
immediately by the prediction of a martyr's death
for Peter. "Verily, verily I say unto thee, When
thou wast young, thou girdedst thyself, and walkedst
whither thou wouldest: but when thou shalt be old,
thou shalt stretch forth thy hands, and another shall
gird thee, and carry thee whither thou wouldest not."
This spake he, says John, signifying by what death
he should glorify God. The early Church took the
words of Christ, especially what he says about Peter
stretching forth his hands, as a prediction that he
would be crucified like his Lord. But whether Christ
meant that or not, he did definitely predict a violent
martyr's death for Peter.

Jesus brought the interview to a close by saying to
Peter, "Follow me." Evidently they had gone apart
somewhat from the other disciples. Peter started to
follow Jesus, and then, seeing that John was ap-

proaching, impulsively curious about what would happen to John, and forgetting for the moment the great commission that Christ had given to him to feed his sheep and to follow his Lord, said, "Lord, and what shall this man do?" This brought Peter another rebuke. Poor, impulsive, warmhearted, stumbling Peter! How many rebukes he had to receive before Christ's training of him was finished! Answering his question about John, Christ said to Peter: "If I will that he tarry till I come, what is that to thee? follow thou me." This last saying of Jesus, as quoted and repeated among the disciples and believers, was by some taken to mean that John would not die, but would be alive when Christ came. The great age to which John did actually live, no doubt added to that impression. But John himself is careful to say that Christ did not definitely predict such a thing for him, but merely said, hypothetically, "If I will," or, "Suppose John does live till I come; what is that to thee?"

Peter is rebuked here for turning his mind away from his one duty to follow Christ and feed his sheep, to fruitless speculation about the fate of his companion apostle John. For all of us the words of Jesus to Peter have as personal a meaning as they did for Peter himself. Always it is our duty and our privilege to follow Christ. Regardless of future events beyond our ken, or present problems beyond

our solution, always the main business is possible—
Follow thou me.

## I. "Follow Thou Me" in Spite of Speculative and Theological Questions

Speculative and theological questions are the most interesting and, in a way, the greatest that can engage the mind of man. Discussion of them may be very profitable; but difficulties involved in them must never obscure the path of duty and of personal relationship to our Lord. The doctrine of the Trinity, that there are three persons in the Godhead, God the Father, God the Son, God the Holy Ghost; and that these three are one God, equal in power and glory, is, in a sense, the foundation truth of Christianity, the article of the standing or falling Church, for it presents to us God as our Creator and Father, God as our Redeemer from sin, and God as our Guide and Inspirer. Yet, when you go beyond that, and try to explain that fundamental and yet mysterious relationship of the Trinity, you attempt the impossible. As Luther said of this grand and sublime truth, "We should, like little children, stammer out what the Scriptures teach: that Christ is truly God, that the Holy Ghost is truly God; and yet that they are not three Gods, or three Beings, as there are three men, three angels, or three windows." After his prolonged treatise on the Trinity, St. Augustine, a great defender of its truth, concludes with a prayer, which he says is better than an argument, and in his prayer he says, "O Lord God, we believe in Thee, the Father, the Son, and the Holy Spirit; for the Truth would not say, Go baptize all nations in the name of the Father, and of the Son, and of the Holy Spirit, unless Thou wast a Trinity."

The problem of evil in this world is another thing which is beyond the explanation of the human mind. God has revealed how man fell, and the results of that Fall we see all about us in the world today. We can believe, too, that evil in the world has been overruled of God for good, for it was sin that brought our Redeemer into the world to die for it, and with him came the most beautiful revelation of the power of the love of God. We can believe, too, that one day Christ shall put every enemy under his feet, and that sin shall be banished from the habitations of man. Still, we cannot say why in the plan of a God of infinite power and goodness sin was permitted. We cannot say why it continues, any more than Robinson Crusoe could answer the question put to him by Friday, when he was giving that savage instruction in Christian truth, "Why does God not kill the devil now?"

Predestination and free will are both taught in the Bible. God orders our path and knows the end from the beginning; and yet in some way we choose, and are held accountable for our choice. Both are rugged, sublime truths, both working in human life. But when you try to reconcile them and see just how they work together, you have a proposition which is too great for the finite human mind. Yet always our duty and our responsibility we know; and ever we can say to ourselves, "*Thou oughtest*."

God's providences are sometimes hard to understand, indeed, sometimes altogether beyond our understanding.

> "God moves in a mysterious way
> His wonders to perform;
> He plants his footsteps in the sea,
> And rides upon the storm." [1]

The other day, I was calling at a home on one of the streets of our city, and just across the street many cars were bringing people to pay their respects at a home where a man had just died, having attained almost a century of life. In the home where I was calling, the married daughter had recently died, leaving an infant of a few months and another child of tender age. Why, you say, could it not have been arranged differently? Why was the old man kept alive far beyond the time when life had satisfaction or joy in it, and the young mother taken from her two babes? Those of us who owe so much to our mothers, we shudder to think how it might have been with us if we had never known a mother.

[1] William Cowper.

Who can answer these questions? They are too high for us; we cannot attain unto them.

There are times when you are troubled about the fate of the unevangelized. Those who think that Christianity is just a collection of maxims of conduct, of good advice, or the way of life, will not be troubled by such questions. But those who believe that it is a faithful saying and worthy of all acceptation that Jesus Christ came into the world to save sinners, and that he told his disciples to go into all the world and preach the gospel to every creature, will have anxious thoughts on this subject. "Whosoever shall call upon the name of the Lord shall be saved. How then shall they call on him in whom they have not believed? and how shall they believe in him of whom they have not heard? and how shall they hear without a preacher?" The man who did the most for the evangelization of the world asks those solemn questions. No surface halfway, trifling Christians of today dare lightly set them aside. And yet how solemn and tremendous are the inferences to be drawn from those questions of Paul.

> "O the generations old,
> Over whom no church bell tolled;
> Christless, lifting up blind eyes,
> To the silence of the skies."

Another great event which has caused endless speculation, and sometimes unhappy disputings, is the very subject which was mentioned by Christ in this last conversation with Peter and John, His Second Coming. It is quite plain that Christ purposely left the time of his coming in the shadow. He might have said very clearly here whether or not he would come during the lifetime of St. John, and thus have prevented misunderstandings and misinterpretations. But, instead of that, he said, "If I will that John tarry till I come, what is that to thee?" At once there arose misunderstanding and misinterpretation concerning the coming of Christ. This has persisted through the ages, and will, no doubt, persist until the hour strikes. We have earnest Christians, who believe that under the present dispensation the world will ripen into a millennial period of righteousness and peace, and then will Christ come; and we have equally earnest premillenarians, who believe that the present age and dispensation, instead of growing to perfection, will wax worse and worse, reaching a fearful climax of iniquity, and then will Christ come to establish the thousand years, or the millennium of peace and joy. Nevertheless, the one great fact that Christ makes clear here and elsewhere, wherever he speaks on this subject, is that he will come. "Occupy till I come," is his charge to his Church; and here again he says to Peter and John, "Till I come." There is no doubt about the coming. But meanwhile, as in the case of Peter, our duty is to prepare for his coming by following him. Whether he is to come in

John's life or not; whether he is to come in your life or not; whether he is to come in this century or not —that you can never know. "What is that to thee? follow thou me."

## II. THE PROBLEMS AND INIQUITIES OF THE WORLD

What is true of the speculative events and of the great theological questions is true of the problems and evils and evil institutions of the world. There is a certain sense in which, when we are too much troubled about these things, Christ can say to us, "What is that to thee? follow thou me." There is a tendency on the part of the Church today to assume responsibilities which belong to God alone.

War is bad. How many millions the Red Horse and his rider have trampled under his iron hoofs from age to age! And now again we see the world armed to the teeth and every evidence of another Armageddon. War is bad, bestial; the defiler of the temple of the Holy Spirit. But the Church is not responsible for war. The Christian Church does not incite men to kill one another, nor does it persuade men to indulge in those sins and lusts whence come wars and fightings among us. If I read the Gospels aright, there will be wars and rumors of war down to the very end. How absurd, therefore, for the Church to take upon herself the responsibility for war, and how absurd to say that Christianity has failed because men do not beat their swords into plowshares or their spears into pruning hooks.

Child labor, unjust industrial and economic conditions, sweatshops, unfair bargaining—all this is bad. But the Church is not responsible for the social order of the world. It is its duty to cry out against these evils, and denounce the doers of them. But Christ never said that the Church was to establish here in this world a perfect social order. Indeed, upon one occasion he peremptorily refused to arbitrate in a case of social injustice, but said to the petitioner, "Man, who made me a judge or a divider over you?"

The moving pictures are bad, with their open or, still worse, attractively disguised nakedness and seduction. The open advocacy of the sex ethics of the stockyard and the barnyard is bad; the prurient stream of popular literature is bad, as bad as anything in the days when the gospel was first preached in the Roman Empire. But the gospel of Christ is not responsible for these things. The Church is not responsible for them. These are evils which inhere in human nature. Christ nowhere says that all evils are going to disappear from the earth before he comes the second time, and there is not a sentence in the New Testament which affords ground for indicting the Church or Christianity as having failed because great and terrible evils still prevail in the earth. On the contrary, Christ makes it plain that he will come to a world shaken with strife, bound in falsehood, and bankrupt in faith. "When the Son of man cometh, shall he find faith on the earth?"

Let us not, then, assume responsibilities which belong to God. This is not our world, but his world. He has placed his Church in the world, and the gates of hell shall not prevail against it. Ours it is to hold up the lamp of truth, to pronounce God's judgments upon a wicked and adulterous generation, and ever to say to Zion, "Thy God cometh." No matter how dark the age, no matter how difficult the day for anyone of us, always it is possible for us to do what Christ told Peter to do when he answered his curious question about John on that memorable morning by the beautiful Sea of Galilee by saying to him, "What is that to thee? follow thou me."

# PETER ON THE MOUNT

## XIII

*"Master, it is good for us to be here: and let us make three tabernacles; one for thee, and one for Moses, and one for Elias"*

Mark 9: 5

A GREAT soul desires to share its great moments with others. In the greatest moments of his life, Jesus had for his companions Peter, James, and John. He took them with him into the chamber of death when he brought to life the daughter of Jairus. They were his companions, although sleeping companions, when he entered into his agony in the Garden of Gethsemane; and when he went up into a high mountain and was transfigured, Peter and James and John were chosen to behold that glory. The only time when Jesus was altogether alone, and when he took none with him, was when he faced temptation and sin in the Wilderness.

All we know about the Mount of Transfiguration is that it was "a high mountain." Tradition has identified the mountain as Mount Tabor, that impressive mountain that rises grandly above the plain of Esdraelon, the battlefield of the ages, and the battlefield which gives St. John his name for the last great conflict between Christ and his enemies, Armageddon. Some, however, think that the mountain must have been one of the ranges of Hermon. But that makes no difference in the power and majesty, the beauty and the instruction, of this great event in the life of our Lord.

After the labor of the day is over, Jesus and the three disciples in the soft evening twilight climb the mountainside, higher and higher, until the sleeping villages are lost to their view. Whether it was Tabor, whence they could look down on the plain of Esdraelon, where Deborah and Barak overthrew the hosts of Sisera, and the mountains of Gilboa where Saul perished, and Nazareth, and the far-off sea, or to the south the mountains about Jerusalem, or to the east the mountains beyond the Sea of Galilee, or some other mountain, it was a suitable theater and stage for the great transaction.

The disciples were weary after their long climb up the mountainside, and, lying down, at once fell asleep. But while they were sleeping Jesus was praying. In his narrative of the Transfiguration Luke says that Jesus went up into the mountain to pray, and that, "as he prayed, the fashion of his countenance was altered, and his raiment was white and glistering." We are much indebted to Luke for that record. It was while he was praying that he was transfigured. Prayer opened the gates of heaven for Christ; and, in a different sense, of course, this is true of man when he prays. It is not in the midst of the political discussion, or the gossip of the social hour, or in the business transaction, that the face of man is ennobled, transfigured, as it were, but when he is praying.

While he was praying the person of Christ was transfigured. All that the Gospels can say about it is that "His face did shine as the sun, and his raiment was white as the light." The sun and the light—in beauty and in glory there is nothing beyond that. But that was not all that happened. Two men, Moses and Elijah, appeared in glory and spake together with Christ; and the disciples, now awakened out of their sleep, saw the glory in the face of their Master and heard Moses and Elijah talking with him. That is another great thing about prayer. It opens unto us the unseen world and puts us in communication with the inhabitants of that world. It is a golden ladder the top of which reaches to heaven. By prayer we climb that ladder and speak with our friends within the veil. It was when St. John was praying, when he was "in the Spirit on the Lord's day," that a window was opened for him into the Heavenly City.

The face of Jesus shining like the sun, the great prophets, Moses and Elijah, talking with him, surely that was enough for one night. But something more wonderful yet was to come. A bright soft cloud for a moment floated over them, and out of the cloud the three disciples heard a voice saying, "This is my beloved Son, in whom I am well pleased." At the sound of that voice Peter and James and John fell to the ground. But Jesus came and touched them, and said, "Arise, and be not afraid." And when they lifted up their eyes again, this time they saw Jesus only. The cloud was gone; the heavenly Voice no longer spake; Moses and Elijah had vanished into the unseen world. They saw no man, save Jesus only.

Today our special interest in the story of the Transfiguration is what Peter had to say about it. What he said was, "Lord, it is good for us to be here; and let us make three tabernacles; one for thee, and one for Moses, and one for Elias." I have read many comments on this utterance by Peter, and listened to sermons that were preached upon this text, and the general tenor of the comments has been that Peter made an absurd and ridiculous utterance; in plain English, he made a fool of himself. Because of his always ready speech, he felt that he had to say something here, although he had no conception of what was going on, and therefore what he uttered was nonsense. Thus we are told that Peter proposed that they stay forever on the mountain top, forget all about the sorrowing and suffering world on the plains below them where the nine disciples were making a futile effort to heal the poor boy who was possessed of a devil. In his selfish delight, unmindful of the needs of a lost world, Peter was going to live with Christ and the great prophets in tabernacles on the mount where he could sit and sing to himself,

> "My willing soul would stay
> In such a frame as this,
> And sit and sing herself away
> To everlasting bliss." [1]

But such an interpretation reads a great deal into the narrative that is not there. However much the preachers and commentators have criticized Peter for what he said here, and ridiculed his desire to stay on the Mount with Christ and the prophets, it is very significant that Jesus, who was always ready to set Peter right when he made, as he sometimes did, a wrong utterance, uttered no word of rebuke. What Peter said was grandly true. It was a moment of great uplift and inspiration for him. His soul was thrilled with the presentation of heavenly truths, with the glory of Christ as the Son of God, with the glimpse he had into the unseen world, with the communion and fellowship with the mighty and glorious dead. What more fitting, therefore, than that he should have exclaimed, "Lord, it is good for us to be here!" What more appropriate and honorable than

[1] Isaac Watts.

that he should express the desire to remain in the mood of that moment, to catch and hold its glory, and to abide in the fellowship of the great prophets, Moses and Elijah. What Peter saw and felt and heard here was, first of all, the glory of Jesus as the Son of God; second, the glory of his atonement; and third, the glory of the life to come.

## I. The Glory of the Son of God

It is very important to remember what the three evangelists who narrate the transfiguration are careful to note, namely, that it was a number of days after the great event at Caesarea Philippi, when in answer to the question of our Lord, "Whom do men say that I am?" and then "Whom say ye that I am?" Peter made his great confession, "Thou art the Christ, the Son of the living God." Immediately after that, to the amazement of Peter, and no doubt of the other apostles also, Jesus had announced that he must suffer many things of the elders and chief priests and scribes, and be killed and be raised again the third day. In spite of the severe rebuke which Christ gave to Peter for his rash, "Lord, this shall not be unto thee," and in spite of his deep and beautiful words spoken at the same time, that "whosoever will lose his life shall find it," and that "whosoever shall save his life shall lose it," the announcement of the Cross, that Christ was to suffer humiliation and death, must have seemed to the Apostles a

[ 141 ]

strange sequel to the declaration of his divine Sonship. For this reason the Transfiguration was a timely event. Peter and James and John, and through them the other disciples, are to learn that Peter's inspired confession, that Christ was the Son of God, was really true. It was confirmed in the glory and beauty of the Transfiguration when they saw his face as the sun, his garment as the light, and heard the Voice out of the cloud saying, "This is my beloved Son, in whom I am well pleased; hear ye him." How the truth of this vision of the glory of Christ sank into the minds of two of those who saw it, Peter and John, we know from what they wrote long afterwards, for John in his Gospel said, "The Word was made flesh, and dwelt among us, and we beheld his glory, the glory as of the only begotten of the Father"; and Peter, in his Second Letter, says that he was an "eyewitness of the majesty of Christ." Then there came such a voice to him from the excellent glory, "This is my beloved Son, in whom I am well pleased. And this voice which came from heaven we heard, when we were with him in the holy mount." The disciples had followed the familiar form of their Master through the streets of Capernaum and along the shores of the Sea of Galilee, they had seen that face suffused with pity and compassion as he stopped on the highway to heal the sick or open the eyes of the blind, or take little children into his arms. But never before had they seen it radiant with the full glory of the Son of God, the glory which he had with the Father before the foundation of the world.

The Christ of the miracles and the parables, the Christ of the highways and byways of Galilee, survives in history only because he is seen in the light of the glory of the Son of God. It is that glory which has kept him before the world. Never altogether obscured to human sight and faith, over the Dead Sea of the world's rejection and hatred and persecution there has floated this vision of his glory. This is why the world has not, cannot, will not forget Christ.

## II. The Glory of the Atonement

Moses and Elijah spake with Christ concerning his decease, or his exodus which he should accomplish at Jerusalem. In other words, they talked with him about the Cross, about the Atonement. We would give a great deal to know what the two great prophets had to say on that greatest of all subjects. The Cross is the central thought of heaven, as it is the one great fact and the one great act on earth. Even his closest disciples, even Peter who was inspired to confess him as the Son of God, could not at that time understand the meaning, the necessity, and the glory of the Atonement, of his coming death for sinners on the Cross. But now, for his encouragement and comfort and delight, God breaks the seals of the unseen world, and Moses and Elijah come forth to talk with Christ about the great work he was to do on the Cross. They let him know that, however indifferent men on earth were as to his passion and death, it was the one subject of thought and hope among the godly dead, among the inhabitants of heaven, and that the angels themselves desire to look into it.

Sometimes I feel that Christ would find himself a little lonely in our churches today. I can imagine him sitting in humble disguise in the churches, and then, when he came out, saying, "They spoke earnestly of me as a Helper, and a Friend, as a Leader of Men, as one who sympathizes with all the oppressed, as one who hates injustice and hypocrisy and war. All that was good, but I waited in vain to hear them speak of that about which Moses and Elijah spoke with me on the Mount, that which is dearest to my heart, and dearest to the heart of my Father in Heaven, how I died on the Cross for their sins."

## III. The Glory of the Future Life

Moses and Elijah appeared in glory and spake with Jesus. Suppose the Gospels had said only that two of the great personalities of the Old Testament appeared in glory and spake with Jesus, what two would you have chosen for that honor? Perhaps Abraham and Isaac, or Jacob and Joshua, or Samuel and Daniel, or Noah and Job, or Isaiah and Jeremiah. Grand personalities, all of them. Yet there was a fitness in the appearance of Moses and Elijah, Moses who wrote of him, whose acts of deliverance of the children of Israel out of Egypt were to be forever a type and prophecy of how Christ delivers his people from the bondage of sin, and Elijah recognized and honored because of his magnificent courage, his heroic witness to the Kingdom of God and to the truth in an age of wickedness and apostasy.

The two prophets as they spoke with Jesus about his death and crucifixion, also by their glory and their very presence, tell us wonderful things and confirm wonderful hopes about the life of the blessed dead within the veil. Moses and Elijah are not reduced to nothingness; neither are they in a state of unconsciousness, or an agelong sleep, waiting for the day of the Resurrection. They appear in all the fullness of their personality, in all their personal identity, with intelligence, with consciousness, with the power of thought and speech, with a living interest in the work of the Redeemer for mankind. The same persons, and yet glorified with the powers of the life to come. Who would go to a seance, who wants the confirmation of crystal gazers, witches of Endor, and table tilters, when here in the Gospels, in the account of the Transfiguration, he has this glorious demonstration of the reality of the life to come and the wonderful powers with which the be-

lieving dead are endowed? With that let us put
away our doubts and comfort our hearts.

> "It is an old belief
> That on some solemn shore,
> Beyond the sphere of grief,
> Dear friends shall meet once more.
>
> Beyond the sphere of time
> And sin and fate's control,
> Serene in changeless prime,
> Of body and of soul.
>
> That creed I fain would keep,
> That hope I'll not forego,
> Eternal be the sleep
> Unless to waken so." [2]

That will be one of the joys of the heavenly life,
to talk with the mighty and glorious dead. If Socrates could look forward with a thrill of expectation
to conversing with Homer and the mighty dead of the
ancient world, how much more the Christian, when
he thinks of talking with Moses and Elijah, with
Peter and John and Paul; but most of all, with the
Lord Jesus Christ himself, for after Elijah and
Moses were gone, the disciples saw Jesus only. As
he was the central figure on the Mount of Transfiguration, so he will be the central figure in Im-

[2] Lockhart.

manuel's land. Not great Moses, nor grand Elijah, nor sweet-singing and deeply sinning David, nor eloquent Isaiah, nor world-conquering Paul, nor John with the music of heaven in his voice, nor Peter to whom we owe more of our knowledge of Christ and of his redeeming love than to any other, and not even the faces which we have loved and lost awhile, and then have found again, and forever, in that blessed land, shall detain our eager and searching gaze; but the Face of Him, whom having not seen, we yet love. And in that great Morning, when we have seen Him, we shall say with ourselves, and to Him and to Peter and James and John and Moses and Elijah, "Lord, it is good for us to be here!" There we shall build the Tabernacles of our joy, never to be taken down, our Eternal Tent in the Land of the Beloved.

# PETER'S "WHAT SHALL WE HAVE?"

## XIV

### *"What shall we have?"*

Matthew 19: 27

*"Verily I say unto you, There is no man that hath left house, or brethren, or sisters, or father, or mother, or wife, or children, or lands, for my sake, and the gospel's, but he shall receive a hundred-fold now in this time, houses, and brethren, and sisters, and mothers, and children, and lands, with persecutions; and in the world to come eternal life."*

Mark 10: 29, 30

O N the wall of the church where I first preached [1] I used to see, when I was sitting in the pulpit, a black marble tablet which had been placed there in memory of two missionaries who had been put to death at Cawnpore by Nana Sahib during the Sepoy Mutiny in 1857. Following the

[1] The First Presbyterian Church, Paterson, N. J.

[ 148 ]

names of the missionaries and the account of their
martyrdom was this passage from Mark's Gospel.
Looking at that monument, I used to wonder about
it; not the final promise—"and in the world to come
Eternal Life"—but the first part of the verse—Re-
ceiving a hundredfold, now in this time, of brethren,
and lands, and relatives.

I thought of the hardships of the six months'
voyage in a sailing vessel around Cape Horn to
India; then the journey into Northern India to Fut-
tehgurh, where they were stationed; then the out-
break of the savage mutiny; their journey down
the Ganges River to Cawnpore under a false promise
of safety; then the dawning of the day of the mas-
sacre; the hours of suspense; the hostile glances of
their captors; then the coming of the blood-intoxi-
cated fanatics, the tearing of the bride from the arms
of her husband; the insults, the imprecations, the
howls of Satanic rage, the torture, the suffering, the
thoughts of friends and home, the thought for one
another; and at the end, the anesthesia of death.

What, then, can be the meaning of this verse on
their memorial tablet in the church that sent them
out? They had given up houses and lands, father
and mother, brethren and sisters for Christ's sake
and the gospel's. But where now was the hundredfold? Instead of that they had received torture and
death at the hands of barbarians. Evidently, then,
in this great promise the words of Jesus are not to

be taken literally. It must be some other kind of houses and lands and brethren and relatives and wives and parents about which he is speaking. Let us see.

Jesus had just concluded one of the most memorable and touching interviews in the history of his ministry. A rich young ruler, interested in Jesus and in Eternal Life, came running to him and asked him, "What shall I do that I may have eternal life?" After questioning him about how he lived in this world, and sounding him out on the Ten Commandments, Jesus put him to a severe test, saying, "If thou wilt be perfect, go and sell that thou hast, and give to the poor, and thou shalt have treasure in heaven: and come and follow me." But when the young man heard that saying he went away sorrowful: for he had great possessions.

Looking wistfully after him, for we are told that He loved him Jesus said to the disciples, "How hard it is for them that trust in riches to enter the kingdom of God. It is easier for a camel to go through the eye of a needle, than for a rich man to enter into the kingdom of God." Astonished at this the disciples exclaimed, "Who then can be saved?" Whereupon Jesus answered, "With men this is impossible; but with God all things are possible." Perhaps Jesus meant to say here that there was hope yet even for this young man who had rejected him. It is a sad thing to see anyone reject Christ, but doubly sad when one who is drawn to Jesus, like this young man, turns away from him and is unwilling to pay the price of discipleship. But whether Jesus meant to hold out a hope here for the rich young ruler, or not, what he said is forever true. Humanly speaking, salvation is never possible; divinely speaking—that is, when we make allowance for the gracious work of God's Holy Spirit—it is *always* possible.

We can imagine the disciples listening in silence to this last word of Jesus. Then Peter speaks up with his question. Always it is Peter who asks the question and gets a great answer. This is what he said: "Lord, we have left all, and have followed thee; what shall we have therefore?" This was equivalent to saying: "This rich young ruler is not willing to leave all and follow thee; but we have done that. Now what shall we have?" None of the disciples was a rich man, but it meant as much for Peter and James and John to leave their nets and their fishing boats as it would have meant for the rich young ruler to sell all that he had and follow Christ.

Here again most preachers and commentators have been quick to condemn Peter and repudiate his question. For example, one says, "How this man drags the stars out of heaven and tramples upon them! How he debases the ideality of life, the prophecy and the apocalypse of human being and education." But the more you meditate upon this passage, the less ready you are rashly to judge and condemn Peter. No doubt there was something of a vagueness in his mind as to what was to be the end of their fellowship with Jesus. No doubt, too, there were mistaken ideas about the Messianic splendor of an earthly kingdom in which they hoped to share. But Peter's question was all right; altogether fitting and appropriate. He wants to know what is to be the end of their faith and discipleship. Long afterwards, when he understood it better, Peter did not need to ask this question; for he said in his First Letter to the persecuted disciples of Jesus, that the end of the disciples' faith was the salvation of his soul. But now the thing is not clearly defined. So far, they had had only long, tiresome journeys along the roads of Galilee and Judea, storms on the Sea of Galilee, days of hunger and thirst, and the hostility of the people. He knew that there was something more than this in store for them; so he said, "Lord, what shall we have?"

In the great answer which he gave him, Jesus spoke, first of all, and in particular, to the Twelve Disciples; and then, in general, to every faithful and self-denying follower of Christ in every age. To the apostles in particular Jesus said: "Verily I say unto you, That ye which have followed me, in the regeneration when the Son of man shall sit in the throne of his glory, ye also shall sit upon twelve thrones, judging the twelve tribes of Israel." Here the thing upon which to center your thought is not the no doubt highly figurative language about the twelve thrones and judging the twelve tribes of Israel, but that great promise and announcement about regeneration. Here Christ declares that all things are to be restored to the original plan and order which God had in mind for man at the creation, only with this difference: that the original and sinless state of man is to be developed into a state of glory and happiness founded upon redemption. That is what the world needs; that is what you and I need—a regeneration, a new birth. That regeneration one day shall come. It will not come through the efforts of man; it will not come through political revolution, or experiments; it will not come through the evolution of human society toward a goal of perfection; it will come when Christ himself shall come to fulfill and establish all righteousness. Compared with the glory and splendor of that day of regeneration, the brightest glory which yet has invested the world is but the shadow of darkness and death.

Now comes the general promise for all who for the sake of Christ and the gospel have preferred him and his gospel to the things of this world; that here, in this time, in this life, and in this age, they shall receive an hundredfold of what they have given up— fathers, mothers, husbands, wives, brethren, sisters, lands, and houses; and in the world to come eternal life. The great promise naturally divides itself into two parts: What the believer in Jesus is to have in this world; and, secondly, what he is to have in the world to come. One of Paul's four faithful sayings is an answer, or a parallel, to these words of Jesus: "Godliness is profitable unto all things, having promise of the life that now is, and of that which is to come." That is exactly what our Lord told Peter and the disciples, that the man who follows him gets the most out of this life and inherits eternal life in the world to come.

## I. Now in This World

The Christian man has high rewards even in this life. Godliness is profitable. We have already seen that our Lord cannot have been speaking literally, for a hundredfold of houses and mothers and wives is manifestly impossible. Something deeper than that lies in the promise of Christ. What, then, are some of the things that the follower of Christ gets in this world?

In the first place, all the possessions, all the relationships, and all the pleasures of life are enlarged, illuminated, and transfigured by Christian faith. Christian faith opens a window and door in every direction. Godliness enlarges the territory of a man's life. The godly man gets more out of business, society, books, science, travel, than any other man. No matter what the calling or the work, he is a stronger and better man in it if he is a godly man. Godliness brings light. It is true, as the old hymn puts it, that godliness "lights up a dying bed," but it also lights up the path of life from day to day. "The path of the just is as a shining light."

Another reward of the godly life in this world is a Good Influence. Here is something that we cannot assume, cannot purchase, and cannot pretend to have if we do not have it. It is the reflection, the echo, of a godly life. This is the influence that comes first among the forces of life. I pause for a moment, and let you think of someone, father or mother, teacher or friend, husband or wife, whose influence has been, and is, one of the strongest, most blessed, and most abiding things in your life. What higher ambition could man have, what greater reward could he seek, than to leave behind him an influence that blesses; like the shadow of this Peter who asked the question of our text, which, when he walked down the streets of Jerusalem, fell in benediction upon the sick?

In this life the follower of Christ has the reward of a Good Conscience. Here is a reward which is not to be discounted. The interrogation of a good conscience is a treasure which cannot be bought in any market on earth. It is the pearl of great price; but the price that we pay for it is faith in Jesus Christ and obedience to his laws. How pathetic it is to see men who are successful, men who are accomplished, men who are brilliant, and yet who do not have the companionship of a good conscience. The world bestows its honors and decorations; but the highest decoration that can ever come to you is the "Well done" of your own conscience. If conscience cannot decorate you, then all the decorations of the world are but tinsel and trash. I suppose Christ had something of that in mind when he said, at the close of his answer to Peter, speaking of the splendors of the rewards of his kingdom and of the day of regeneration, that many that are first shall be last, and the last shall be first. That is to say, that many whom the world has envied and honored will be lost sight of altogether, and humble, unheralded, but faithful doers of the will of God shall take the first rank in the kingdom of God.

## II. And in the World to Come

You never hear Christ preach without striking that chord, which, alas, is the lost chord of much of our teaching and preaching today. Christ speaks as a man whose eyes are ever fixed on that life beyond the margin of this life. "And in the world to come." The less men think about that world to come, the sadder they make, and the weaker, their own life; and the more terrible they make this world.

We have seen how, as Paul put it, that godliness has the promise of the life that now is; that a godly man gets more out of this world than any other man. But that is not all: it has the promise also of that which is to come. You might say, therefore, that the follower of Jesus has in this life the kindly light of a great hope for the future, and that in the life to come he enters into the fullness of Eternal Life. There the Christian man always has the great advantage over every other man. In a famous letter, writing to the husband of an English lady who had sent him a prayer for the poet's salvation which had been found among her papers, Lord Byron, speaking of the hope of the future, says: "*Indisputably, the firm believers in the Gospel have a great advantage over all others—for this simple reason, that, if true, they will have their reward hereafter; and if there be no hereafter, they can be but with the infidel in his eternal sleep, having had the assistance of an exalted hope through life without subsequent disappointment, since (at the worst of them) 'out of nothing nothing can arise,' not even sorrow.*"  [2]

There is, indeed, something in that; yet it hardly agrees with what the Apostle said, that if in this world only we have hope in Christ, we are of all men most miserable. No matter how learned, honored, or prosperous a man may be, if he has no hope for the future he is a sad spectacle, for nothing is more certain than that life passes. The years draw nigh when we have no pleasure in them, the sun and the moon and the stars are darkened, the clouds return after the rain, and they that look out of the windows

[2] Dick's *Philosophy of the Future State*, p. 264. E. C. & J. Biddle, Philadelphia, 1867.

are darkened. When the silver cord is loosed and the golden bowl is broken, and the pitcher broken at the fountain, and the wheel broken at the cistern, and all that this life has to offer and all that it can give is over, and nothing more now can be drawn out of its well, what then?

Here the disciple of Jesus has what Peter afterwards called a Living Hope. "Blessed be God, who hath begotten us again unto a Living Hope, by the resurrection of Jesus Christ from the dead, to an inheritance incorruptible, and undefiled, and that fadeth not away." Now Peter knows the rewards and the joys of a follower of Christ in this world, "with persecutions," and the grand hope of the inheritance beyond the skies.

Jesus wept. That is the shortest and one of the deepest verses of the Bible. Why did Jesus weep as he stood by the grave of Lazarus? The Jews thought it was the sorrow of affliction, for they said, "Behold how he loved him!" Yet how could he weep for Lazarus, just when he was about to say, "Lazarus, come forth"? Some again have fancied that Jesus wept and groaned in spirit thinking of the terrible injury that sin had done to the world, of which the death of Lazarus and every other death is an example. But is there a possibility that the reason Jesus wept was this—because Lazarus was in eternal life, in the kingdom of the blessed, with its unspeakable, and to you and me unimaginable, joys, and now, for the present purpose of his kingdom, it was necessary for him to call Lazarus out of that blessed world and back into this world of trial and struggle and probation?

"And in the world to come eternal life!" There we leave it, in the simple but majestic words of Jesus, until in the morning of the Resurrection, in the Day of Regeneration, we shall enter into its joys, the greatest of which, we know beyond the peradventure of a doubt, will be the joy of the presence of that Saviour who loved us and died for us.

# PETER'S SHADOW

## XV

### *"That at the least the shadow of Peter passing by might overshadow some of them"*

Acts 5: 15

HE was a young man who undoubtedly belonged to Christ. But only in the last part of his life had he given himself to Christ. When he came to die, he was filled with regret that he had done so little for Christ, and with remorse that he had done so much against him. His dying request was this, "Bury my influence with me."

That was a will and testament which could not be executed. Suppose his executors had tried? How could they have laid hands on that man's influence and buried it in his grave with him? There are multitudes of men who could wish that they could cancel and nullify their influence, and who when they come to die, even though trusting in the forgiving mercy of Christ, will regret that they cannot take their influence down into the grave with them.

In the Book of Acts we are told that when Peter

was healing the sick, those who were unable to get near him for the press of the crowd, so that he might heal them by the touch of his hand, were laid by their friends along the street, so that when Peter passed by, his shadow might fall on them and heal them. It may be inferred, although it is not directly stated, that some of the sick were healed in this way by the shadow of Peter falling upon them. If so, it is a miracle no greater than if he had touched them with his hand, because the healing power was supernatural. So far as nature is concerned, there was as much healing power, or as little, in the shadow of Peter as there was in the touch of his hand. The God who could use the touch of a hand to heal a sick man could just as easily use the touch or the reflection of a shadow.

As Peter passed up and down the streets of Jerusalem he cast a shadow on one side or the other. As you go up and down the streets of life, passing the sick, the wounded, the sorrowful, the glad, the jubilant, you cast always a shadow. There is one self that you carry about with you, and that other self, the shadow self which has touched the lives of others. What a strange thing a shadow is! Immaterial, insubstantial, yet it gives the image of the real. Riding through the country on a railway train on a bright winter day, you have noticed that every object casts its shadow—the train in which you were riding, the smoke pouring from the engine, the barn, the tree, the fences, the cattle, birds circling in the air, animals grazing in the field. All things, animate and inanimate, cast their shadow. So as we go through life, always an influence falls from us, as noiselessly, but as inevitably, as irrevocably as the shadow.

"This, learned I, from the shadow of a tree
Which to and fro did play upon the garden wall,
Our shadow selves, our influence may fall
Where we ourselves may never be." [1]

Now and then, we are confronted by the record of our shadow, and are startled to see how it has healed or blighted, how it has comforted or wounded. The men of whom Jesus spake were surprised in the day of judgment, both the good and the bad, because the Judge opened their eyes and let them see the effects of their shadow selves as they walked along the paths of life.

## I. Unconscious Influence

We may influence others when we are making an earnest and deliberate effort to do so. But ofttimes our most effective and abiding influence will be unconscious. When this same Peter ran with John to the sepulcher on the day of the Resurrection when they heard the tidings that the grave was empty, "that other disciple"—that is, John—being the

[1] Anne Hamilton.

younger and the more active, did outrun Peter, and
came first to the tomb. But he feared to enter in,
and was hesitating at the mouth of the tomb, when
Peter came toiling up and in his impulsive manner
went at once into the tomb and saw how it was empty.
"Then entered in also that other disciple, and believed." Peter was not thinking of influencing John
when he hurried into the sepulcher; but his courageous act was contagious and stirred John into action
and brought him to a belief in the resurrection of his
Lord.

Henry Ward Beecher, in one of his sermons, testi-
fies that one of the chief influences of his life, in the
early formative, critical period of his life, was a
Negro hired man who worked at his side on his
father's farm. The Negro never deliberately tried,
by act or by word, so far as Beecher could see, to
influence him, but patient, worthy Christian manhood
all the time was making its impress upon the young
life at his side. When the disciples saw Jesus so
earnest and fervent in his prayers, then it was that
they besought him to teach them "how to pray," and
the answer was the Lord's Prayer. Every man,
Emerson once said, is an oracle to some one else.
Where you may little imagine it or think it, the
shadow of your character and personality is falling.
What kind of a shadow is it?

Once passing through the corridors of a great
hospital, I saw sitting on a bench a minister whom I

had known. He was a man well advanced in years,
now broken in health, and for some time had given
up his church, where he had been in unhappy dis-
putes with members of his congregation. I turned
to speak with him, expecting to hear from him some
word of melancholy reminiscence or present gloom;
but I received a pleasant surprise. He told me that
a woman going by had just turned to speak with
him and had told him that long ago a word spoken
by him in the pulpit had been the means of bringing
her to Christ. He was happy in the knowledge that
his shadow had once pointed the way to Jesus Christ.

A rose exhales its sweet odor simply because it is
a rose. The best way to be sure of exerting a benefi-
cent and beautiful influence is to be a genuine sincere Christian. No one can be that without virtue,
as Christ said, proceeding from him. Wherever his
shadow falls, men feel the touch and the encouragement of its blessing. When Charles Dickens was
passing one day through the streets of York an unknown woman accosted him saying, "Mr. Dickens,
will you let me touch the hand that has filled my
house with many friends?" Such, then, are the be-
neficent results of the shadow of a good life or a good
work, or a good word, even when the doer or the
speaker thereof is unconscious of it.

But there is also the other kind of influence, ofttimes unconscious too. It would be a good thing for
men to stop and try to follow, if they could, their

shadow. Years ago, when I was a Junior in the Theological Seminary at Princeton, the venerable Dr. William Paxton, once pastor of this church, was just closing his career as a professor. He told us one day of an incident in this church which I have never forgotten. On Sabbath evenings he had noted a young man of fine appearance sitting in one of the galleries, and giving careful and reverent attention to the preacher. Shortly before a Communion season, this man called at Dr. Paxton's home and said he wished to make a confession of his faith and unite with the Church. After the conversation was over, and the arrangement had been made, just as the man was leaving, Dr. Paxton asked, not out of curiosity, but as a matter of courtesy, what his business was. He was surprised when the man told him that he was a liquor dealer and gave the name of one of the best-known breweries or distilleries in Pittsburgh. Dr. Paxton asked him to sit down again and expressed his sorrow that such was the case, explaining to him that with the convictions he held he could not conscientiously receive him into the membership of the Church. But he told him that there was then no Church law on the subject, that it was his own personal judgment in the matter and that there were other ministers whose opinions he did not judge, who took a different view of the matter. The young man replied warmly that he considered the minister's attitude a personal affront. His father and his grand-

father before him had been in the liquor business and
he had always regarded it as an honorable calling.
With an air that told plainly that he was through
with churches and ministers, he took his hat and
walked out. Dr. Paxton never expected to see the
man again. He was therefore much surprised when
one morning several months afterwards the same man
came to his study and said, "Dr. Paxton, when you
refused to receive me as a member of your church
I felt angry and outraged, and resolved in my heart
to have nothing more to do with Churches. But when
I was leaving, you told me that it would be a good
thing if I would see what my business was doing in
the city. The other day I took your advice. I followed one of our wagons about over the city. I
watched it as it went into the private home, the
mansion of the rich, the hovel and the tenement of
the poor, the rich man's club, and the saloon, the poor
man's club, the dance hall, and the places of amusement and of crime. Now I know what you meant.
You were right and I was wrong. I honor and respect you, sir, for refusing to receive me into the
membership of your church. But now that I have
seen the evils of this business, I have given it up, and,
confessing my sins, I desire to be received into the
Church."

It would be a good thing if some men would follow
their shadow for a single day. They might be surprised at the places and the persons where it falls,

and the way in which it falls. What about your shadow in the home, in the street, at the place of business as a Christian man, as a member of Christ's church? Is your shadow such as would commend the gospel? or is it the shadow which would make men say that they would have nothing to do with a gospel professed and confessed by such a man?

A good influence may be destroyed by a bad shadow. The world is filled with people who are so careless and indifferent about the shadow which they cast and the influence which they exert, that when, in some moment of better aspiration and higher purpose, they desire to exert a good influence and cast a helpful shadow, they find that it is impossible to do so. The dark shadow eclipses what they would now do or say. When Lot pleaded with his sons and daughters to flee from the wicked city of Sodom, he seemed to them as one that mocked. There is a deeper meaning in that brief record than is at first apparent on the surface. It is not merely that the sons-in-law and the daughters of Lot thought that he was beside himself with undue fear, or crazed by apprehension of coming cataclysm or catastrophe; not that merely, but that his own life, first pitching his tent toward Sodom, and then dwelling in Sodom, ruined his effectiveness as a preacher. His daily life was such that his own relatives would not take him seriously when he spoke to them about the impending judgments of Almighty God. "He seemed to them as one that mocked." Even an apparently trivial fault, what may seem but a light inconsistency, a moment's loss of self-control, will serve to ruin with some soul the influence of an otherwise good life. Divine grace can remedy these defects of character and overcome them, but even Divine grace will not cancel their unfortunate influence. "That man might preach from morning till evening and speak with the tongues of men and angels, but he could never influence me," said one of a minister from whose lips he had heard unworthy words. The man was good, sincere, his message true; but there was one person to whom he seemed as one that mocked. As one that mocked! If the business men here tonight spoke to their clerks about God and the soul and judgment, would they take you seriously? Or would you seem to them as one that mocked? If the mistress spoke to her maid, would the maid remember acts of unkindness, or those little revelations of human nature which we make nowhere save in the privacy of our home? If the workman spoke to his fellow workman, how would it be? If the student spoke to his roommate, how would it be? If the friend spoke to his boon companion, how would it be? Would he be to them "as one that mocked"?

## II. The Irrevocableness of Our Shadow

A bird flying through the heaven, a cloud floating in the sky, a branch waving in the afternoon breezes, casts a shadow and that shadow it can never recall. So the shadow of human life has an unchangeable and irrevocable aspect about it which is very arresting and solemn. When a stone has been cast into a placid lake or pool, the circles of eddies keep on spreading and multiplying long after the stone which created them has sunk to the bottom of the pool. So, the eddies or circles of our influence, the word, the thought, the deed which has gone out from us keeps moving on, and we can no more stop them or recall them than the stone in the bottom of the lake can stop the circles of eddies which are spreading rapidly across the face of the water. This is true of the good influence as well as the bad. Ian Maclaren, Dr. John Watson, when a boy lost his mother, for whom he had a deep devotion. When she was on her deathbed he made with her some mysterious pact or covenant which he was to keep till they met again in the other world. He used to tell his friends how that sacred treaty and covenant between his mother and himself had often kept him safe when assailed by the temptations of life. There was an influence which nothing in time or eternity could revoke, disannul, or cancel. Likewise Thomas Carlyle in his *Sartor Resartus* describes under other names his boyhood home in Ecclefechan and his mother and father. There he says of his mother: "She did me one altogether invaluable service. She taught me less in deed by word, as by act and daily reverent look and habitude, her own simple version of the Christian faith. The highest whom I knew on earth I saw bowed down with awe unspeakable before a Higher in heaven."

But if a blessed influence sustained by a consistent life remains to the end, so also is the shadow of an evil deed or an evil life irrevocable. One of the sad facts in English poetry is the story of the great Elizabethan poet, John Donne, who in his later life was dean of St. Paul's Cathedral, an eloquent and powerful preacher. In his preaching men noticed a vein of sadness and melancholy. The reason for this sad and minor note in the great preacher's utterances was the fact that in his earlier life he had written and published poems which were filled with the licentiousness and moral putrescence of his age. Now he had given himself to a different message and reasoned with men of righteousness and temperance and judgment to come; but always his preaching was shadowed and haunted by the recollection of those filthy verses which he had once composed and scattered to the world, and which no regret and no repentance could ever recall. He realized that he must influence the world, not only as a preacher of the gospel, but as the author of corrupt and licentious verses.

A man once had a dream and found himself in hell. When he awakened out of the dream he was asked to give an account of what he had seen. Were there flames there? Did he hear horrid oaths of blas-

phemy? "Yes," he said, "but something far worse
than that." "What?" "I was compelled to face my
influence. I knew that I had lived a Godless, wicked
life, and that I deserved punishment, for I had
scorned and rejected Jesus Christ; but my sorest
pain was to see what the effect of my life had been on
others. I saw men come to Hell, worn out with their
sinful indulgences, and among them a man, once a
young man, whom I had influenced toward that end.
I saw souls with all the beauty of their spiritual
birthright gone, withered, wasted, scarred, and I
trembled to learn that they took their first wrong
step following me. I saw a woman despoiled of
woman's beauty and innocence, turned into a fallen
angel, and she, to my horror, said that if she had
never known me she would now be in heaven instead
of hell. I saw men whose minds were full of hatred
and blasphemy against God, who spoke of him in a
way that terrified me, blasphemer though I was; and
some of them recalled words of mine spoken against
the Bible, against faith in God and Christ. Yes, for
me, that will be hell."

The time will come for you and me when all that
we leave behind us, so far as this life is concerned,
will be our influence. What will it be like? Will it
be like that of the young man whose dying prayer
was, "Bury my influence with me"?

# PETER'S "I HAVE NEVER"

## XVI

### *"Lord, I have never"*

#### Acts 10: 14

AT first you can hardly tell whether it is cloud or land, the heavens or the earth, at which you are looking. But as the ship comes closer in, what seems to be cloud takes the form of the hills. Soon the shipping of the harbor appears; and back of the harbor rises the town, with its white and brown houses and their flat roofs. One has a thrill that comes never again—the first view of the Holy Land. There comes a ship out of the harbor, bound for Tarshish, with disobedient Jonah asleep in the hold; and yonder, on the top of that house by the seashore, Peter lies on the roof, dreaming a dream which is to have incalculable influence upon the history of Christianity.

Men speak of the paintings of the Greek-Spanish artist known as El Greco, and how his heavy strokes tell you that what you are looking at is one of El Greco's paintings, in whatever gallery you may see it. So Peter is always Peter, whether in a state of nature or a state of grace; whether before or after he became a follower of Christ; whether during the days of his discipleship or the days of the founding of the Church; whether pulling in nets on the Sea of Galilee, or with Christ in the desert place when he asked them who he was; or listening to Christ talk with Moses and Elijah on the Mount of Transfiguration; or sitting with Christ at the Last Supper; or even in his dreams. You can't miss him or mistake him for any other. No matter where you put Peter down, he will always speak and act like Peter. Nothing could have been more characteristic of Peter than what he said in his dream; that curious mixture of reverence and impertinence, "Not so, Lord; I have never—"

God has strange ways of bringing souls to hear the gospel and to believe in Christ. He has said, "I am sought of them that asked not for me; I am found of them that sought me not." This is true; but also the converse, that God reveals himself to those who search for him. "They that seek me shall find me." In this story we have two visions, or dreams, and a beautiful timing of them. The devout, charitable, and in every way worthy centurion, Cornelius, in his daily prayer at the ninth hour, saw an angel coming to him, who said to him, "Thy prayers and thine alms are come up for a memorial before God. And now send men to Joppa, and call for one Simon, whose surname is Peter: he lodgeth with one Simon a tanner, whose house is by the seaside: he shall tell thee what thou oughtest to do." In obedience to this vision, Cornelius dispatched two servants and a soldier to Joppa, where Peter was lodging. The next day, just as these three men were drawing nigh to Joppa, Peter, at the sixth hour, went up on top of the house to pray. It evidently had been a long time since Peter had dined; and while they made ready below, Peter, very hungry, fell into a trance; and in his trance he saw heaven opened, and a great sheet, as it were, let down to the earth wherein were all manner of four-footed beasts of the earth, and wild beasts, and creeping things, and fowls of the air; and there came a voice, saying, "Rise, Peter; kill, and eat." But Peter answered, "Not so, Lord; for I have never eaten anything that is common or unclean." And the voice spake unto him, "What God hath cleansed, that call not thou common." Peter, now awakened out of his trance, was trying to think what that dream could mean, when there came a knock at the door below; and lo, the three men whom Cornelius had sent came asking if one Peter were lodged there. The next day, Peter went with the three men to Cornelius at Caesarea. When he heard the story of Cornelius, and about his dream, then Peter understood the meaning of what he had seen in the trance. The invitation and command for him to eat things which formerly no Jew was permitted to partake of, let him see that this was a preparation for a command and invitation to preach the gospel to a Gentile. Peter now understood that the gospel was not only for Jews, but for all men; and that in every nation he that feareth him and worketh righteousness is accepted with him. When Peter had delivered his brief sermon, Cornelius and his companions were baptized and received into the faith of the Christian Church.

With that vision of Peter, and the baptism of Cornelius, the gospel took an immense stride forward and assumed its true colors as a universal faith. If anyone should say, too, that all that is necessary is to lead a good, honest, moral life, as it is called, and that it is not necessary to believe in Christ as a Saviour, the best answer is Cornelius. The first Gentile convert is not a robber, murderer, thief, or man of bad character, but this devout man, one that feared God with all his house, and to him by a series of extraordinary steps the Holy Ghost brings the tidings of salvation.

But this morning we turn aside from the major lesson of this beautiful narrative to look for a little at that curious answer of Peter. When he saw the unclean beasts in the sheet and heard the command to rise, kill, and eat them, Peter, in spite of the fact that he was very hungry, said, "Not so, Lord; I have never eaten anything common or unclean, and that is forbidden by the ceremonial law, in all my life."

So far, so good; you must give Peter credit for

standing up for his religious convictions, even when
to set them aside would have gratified the craving
of his body. But now he is to be taught that the
old ceremonial laws do not hold; and that so far as
eating is concerned, one animal is just as clean as
another; and this in turn was to prepare his mind
for the preaching of the gospel to the Gentiles. It
was God's word that Peter seemed to hear; yet
quickly, impulsively, and in a characteristic mingling
of reverence and of impudence, Peter says, "Not so,
Lord; for I have never done it before." Thus the
willfulness of Peter, had he persisted in it, would
have stood in the way of his great usefulness at this
critical period.

Habit and custom and precedent, the reluctance
to do a thing simply because we have never done it
before, often holds up important movements and
frustrates worthy undertakings. "I have never—"
is an alibi or an excuse with which one can refuse
duty and opportunity.

I have often thought how this is true in connection
with personal talent and ability. The more I see of
human nature, the more I wonder at its capacity,
and realize that God did not have time to make no-
bodies. We go generally on the assumption that a
person might be able to do one thing well. He has
capacity, we say, along this line or that line. But
perhaps he can do more than one thing. You have
seen in the newspapers and the magazines the ad-

vertisement of some school of writing or composition, in which an imaginary applicant says he can't write and has never done it; and the answer given is that he has never tried; that he may be able to write just as well as someone else; and there is much in the proposition. Some people say they could never play an instrument, or sing a song; you have to be born to do that. But undiscovered and latent talent may exist where you least suppose it. Someone said to me, "I wish I could hold an audience for three quarters of an hour." I answered, "Perhaps you can. You've never tried it; and you don't know whether you can or not until you've tried it." Underneath the drab and ordinary surface of human nature lies the gold of ability and talent. But in many cases it is never brought to the surface because the working principle of so many people is summed up in this rejoinder of Peter, "I have never—"

Take it now in the field of morals and religion. Here is one who has come into the church and rejoices to a degree in its message and in its presence in the earth; but who may be classed as just a spectator. I remember people telling me once in a former church, both of them very friendly and very interested, that they were "just spectators." But why were they just spectators? Why did they take it for granted that others would assume burdens of responsibility and of support and maintain the activities and the witness of the Church? Largely on the ground of Peter, "Not so, Lord; I have never—"

Then there are these great Christian causes. I pay my portion to the church, my pew rent, or my general contribution. True, it is a small amount compared with what I spend on cosmetics, or hats, or cigars, or the moving picture show, or the tires for my automobile; and yet, it is something; and I am told that even in the churches there are a great many who do nothing. But when you ask me about those great Christian causes, what you call Benevolences, the Christian Colleges and Seminaries, the Home and Foreign Missionary Work, the Korean Club, and so on, I don't feel any responsibility about that. No; I would not have them stopped or crippled in their work; but I sort of take for granted that the Rockefellers and the Harknesses and others will look after the Christian Colleges; and as for these other causes, those who have been accustomed to help them will do so in the future. I can't take it up now. I never put these things on my budget. "Not so, Lord; I have never—"

And what about that Sunday-school class? Yes, I think it's a great work, and a fine thing to have children and young people and adults meeting together every week to study the Bible; and it must be a fine thing to be the teacher of a class.

But me! a class for me! why, surely you don't mean

that? I have never done anything like that. I don't know enough about the Bible.

But the Bible is worth knowing, and you will learn more about it teaching a Sunday-school class in a month than you would in ten years otherwise.

But there are some things in my life, some little habits—not altogether bad, you understand—but just some things that might be thought not to fit in with teaching a Sunday-school class.

Then drop them! What are the dregs of the ill-odored cup of the world's pleasures compared with the abiding joys and satisfactions of God's service? When all that which belongs to the world and your personal indulgences has withered, faded, vanished, turned to nothing, the influence, the currents of action which you may have set in motion in some humble Sunday-school class, will be moving throughout all eternity.

And there is that Sunday evening service.

Yes, I've heard about it, and in this day when the old habit of churchgoing has been given up in so many places, and when the Sunday evening service is being abandoned by so many churches, I think it's a great thing to know that a church in the center of the city is filled on a Sunday night and that the gospel is preached to so many people. You can never estimate the results which flow from such a service as that; the discouraged or the despairing who are given hope, the tempted who are warned, the wandering who are recalled, and the lost who are found. Yes, it's a great thing. Keep it up by all means. But you ask me, Do I go? Will I be there tonight? Why, no; I'm afraid not. I just go on the assumption that somebody else will be there. I've always gone to church Sunday morning, but not on Sunday night. That's the night we drive out to visit my wife's mother. "No, not so, Lord; I have never—"

And there are the different missionary organizations and societies.

No; I wouldn't have them give up their work, that would be too bad. I think we ought to obey what Christ said in his last message to the Church, "Go ye into all the world, and preach the gospel to every creature." If any Church member thinks he knows better than Christ, then he has advanced pretty far, and ought to have a church and a religion of his own. But will *I* be there at the meeting this month, or at those on Monday night? No, I'm afraid not. I have never gone to those meetings. That's the night my husband's uncle comes to dinner, and we have to get ready for him. "Not so, Lord; I have never—"

And there is that Wednesday night meeting.

That's a good thing, too. My father and mother never missed, and father made a prayer every week. I hate to hear of churches giving up their prayer meetings. It always looks to me as if the Holy Spirit was about ready to depart from such a church.

It's a fine thing to have those meetings with praise and intercession and the explanation of the Scriptures; and it gives the people a chance, too, to become acquainted with one another. But me! why, you didn't really expect me to come, did you? O no; the minister would fall off his platform if he saw me come in on Wednesday night. "Not so, Lord; I have never—"

And there is the Tuesday Noon Meeting for Business Men.

Yes, I have heard about that meeting. Our pastor announces it every Sunday and urges the men to come. I hear good reports of it, too. I think it is a great thing to have so many men meet together at noon in the middle of the week to praise God and talk together about the Kingdom of Christ and the welfare of their immortal souls. By all means, let the good work go on. But I? Will I be there next Tuesday? No; I'm afraid not. I always take lunch at the Club on Tuesday. We have the same table every week. No, it would not do to break that up, even for the sake of Christ and the Church. If I don't go there, I go down to ———'s restaurant for a sauerkraut luncheon. No; I guess I'll not be there next Tuesday. "Not so, Lord; I have never—"

In this case, Peter's "I have never—" almost kept him from preaching the gospel to Cornelius and bringing a soul to Christ. Do you know what Christ said, not only to his disciples but to you and me just before he was taken up into heaven? It was this— "Ye shall be my witnesses."

I believe that, and I'll support the ministers and stand by the churches to the last. I'm ready to stand up and tell the Bolshevik and the atheist and the church persecutor just what I think of him, any time and any place. But as for being a direct witness, speaking to someone myself, no, I'm afraid I could not do that; I have never done it.

Then it is time to begin. Try it, and see how it will give the ring of reality to your religion and your faith. You can speak to that friend about Japan and China, about the stocks, about the mildest winter in fifty years—what about a word in behalf of his soul, a word for Christ? "They that be wise shall shine as the brightness of the firmament; and they that turn many to righteousness as the stars forever and ever."

Here is a man who looks not with hostility, but even with wistfulness on the Church and the Christian faith. But the definite stand, the confessing the Lord Jesus Christ with my mouth, that I have never done. Some day I may do it, but not now. "Not so, Lord; I have never—" No; I don't think I'm too good a man to need the cleansing of Christ's blood; but to stand up before a congregation and confess that, to repent of my sins and to pray to God, "God be merciful to me a sinner," no, "Not so, Lord; I never have—"

So to life's great opportunities and most important duties, men say No; and too often on this ground, "Lord, I have never—" But now the soul is about to be confronted with a new experience, something altogether unknown in its experience. Now comes the messenger who cannot be bribed; now approaches the herald of the end, and the great change. Lord, give me one more chance! Surely, Thou wilt do that! Turn back the shadow on the dial, Lord, and give me five years, or even one year, Lord, and I'll show my minister what it is to be a real worker and helper in the Church and in Christ's Kingdom. Thou surely wilt not take me away without another chance. And those people, Lord, whom I might have helped or encouraged, and to whom I might have spoken a word in season, if Thou wilt only give me another opportunity, I will certainly do it. And those people who were sick or hungry or athirst, and I didn't help them, not because I did not sympathize with them, but because I always found it hard to express myself in that way. I am sorry now, Lord, that I didn't do more, and if Thou wilt give me one more chance, I'll go back and it will be altogether different. And that friend, or partner, or employee of mine I'll talk to him now, Lord. If Thou wilt only give me another opportunity, I'll talk to him now about something more important than the stocks or the weather. And my own habits, and some of them very bad; I'll change them, and then those things which I might have done something to amend, and those words of repentance or restitution or gratitude which I might have spoken, Lord, and am sorry now that I did not, just give me one more chance, Lord, and I will do it. Surely you're not going to take me now—now that I see things so differently. Surely Thou wilt not be harsh and unjust like that. But the answer comes, "This night thy soul shall be required of thee."

And the soul, out it goes, and up it goes, to the great place of examination and the great day of reckoning; and all that those in heaven, on earth, among spirits, or among men can hear, is that sentence of hopelessness and wasted opportunity, "Lord, I have never—"

# PETER AND CORNELIUS

## XVII

*"Who shall tell thee words, whereby thou
and all thy house shall be saved"*

Acts 11: 14

GOD sometimes moves in
a mysterious way to perform the wonders of His
grace. The story of the conversion of the Roman
officer, Cornelius, fixes our attention, not only upon
the fact that this soldier bowed at the feet of the
Prince of Peace, but also upon the wonderful way
in which he was brought to hear of the gospel. The
story of his conversion naturally divides itself into
three parts: first, the congregation and the preacher,
and the way in which they were brought together;
and second, the sermon which was preached; and
third, the results of the sermon and its far-reaching
implications.

### I. THE CONGREGATION AND THE PREACHER
### AND HOW THEY WERE BROUGHT
### TOGETHER

Cornelius was a centurion; that is, the commander
of the sixtieth part of a Roman legion, or one hun

dred men. He was stationed at Caesarea, which was the seat of the Roman government in that part of Syria. His company, perhaps made up of crack troops, was known as the Italian Band. All the associations and all the environment of Cornelius were against his being a good man and a man of faith. His business was that of war. Yet, so placed, Cornelius was a good man.

Too much is made today of heredity and environment, and too many faults and transgressions are condoned or excused on that account. There are, indeed, some people so situated that religious faith and character, humanly speaking, are unlikely, if not impossible; whereas others are so situated that good character and religious faith would seem to be almost inevitable. Yet there are plenty of instances where men have failed utterly in spite of a favorable environment; and other instances where men have come to nobility of character and greatness of faith in spite of a very unfavorable environment. Joseph in the house of Potiphar did not sink to the low level of that house, but rose far above it like a star over the ocean. Obadiah in the house of Ahab and Jezebel did not yield to his environment and become a prophet of Baal, but remained a prophet of the true God. Daniel in the court of Nebuchadnezzar defiled neither his body with the king's meat nor his soul with the customs of that wicked court; and when

Paul preached the gospel at Rome there were saints in Caesar's household.

In spite of his official position and all the temptations that went with it, Cornelius appears before us as a devout man and one that feared God with all his house, who gave much alms to the people, and prayed to God always. He was therefore a just man, charitable, devout, and prayerful. One day at the ninth hour, as he was praying, an angel of God came to him and said to him; "Cornelius!" The devout aspirations of Cornelius had no doubt prepared his soul to receive a special revelation. The great movements in a work of conversion are all on God's side. The truth is generally revealed like a flash of light; yet it is revealed to those who have, all unknown to themselves, for a long time been preparing to receive that revelation. Nor need we wonder that in this case God made use of dreams or visions. Shakespeare in several cases puts the deepest moral experiences of bad men and bad women into their dreams. Why, therefore, should it be thought strange that the greatest moral experiences of good men should have come to them in their dreams?

The angel assured Cornelius that his prayers and his alms had not been unnoted of God. He said to him, "Thy prayer is heard." We take from this that Cornelius had been praying for a higher religious experience, a closer approach to God, and a deeper sense of peace and forgiveness. Here Christ answers His own great beatitude, "Blessed are they that hunger and thirst after righteousness: for they shall be filled."

Cornelius is directed to send messengers to Joppa, where they are to ask for one Simon, surnamed Peter, who was lodging in the house of Simon the tanner, by the seaside. "Peter," said the angel, "will tell thee words, whereby thou and all thy house shall be saved." Nothing doubting, and yet perhaps wondering what it all meant, Cornelius dispatched two servants, together with a trusted soldier, to go to Joppa and ask for Peter.

Now the scene shifts from Caesarea to Joppa. At the sixth hour Peter goes up on the housetop to pray. From his place of prayer, he can see the sleeping sea, the flat-roofed houses of Joppa, and the hills beyond. It was some time since Peter had eaten, and he became very hungry. While he was waiting he fell into a trance. In his vision he saw heaven open, and a great sheet, in which were all manner of animals and creeping things and fowls of the air, was let down to the earth. Then he heard a voice saying, "Rise, Peter; kill, and eat." But Peter responded, "Not so, Lord; for I have never eaten anything that is common or unclean." How characteristic that answer is of Peter; a strange combination of devotion and worship, and yet self-will and disobedience. It is a note which we hear echoing all through the great

apostle's life. When Jesus, after Peter had acknowl-
edged him to be the Son of God, told his disciples
of the humiliation and death of the Cross, Peter began to rebuke him, saying, "Lord, this shall not be
unto thee." So even down to the time of his great
apostolic ministry, Peter is the man who will call Jesus, Lord, and yet question his commandments.

Three times the sheet was let down and then
drawn up into heaven while a voice said, "What God
hath cleansed, that call not thou common." Peter,
now awakened out of his dream, was wondering what
it all meant when he heard the knocking on the door
of Simon by the three messengers who had come from
Cornelius. When he went down to them the messengers told him that they had been sent by Cornelius
to bring him to their Master. The next day Peter
went with them, and at Caesarea was greeted by
Cornelius, who fell at his feet to worship him. Peter
told him to stand up, saying, "I myself also am a
man," with the inference that God alone was worthy
of worship. As if to excuse himself for his presence
in this pagan company, Peter said to Cornelius and
his family and neighbors who had come in also, that
although it was unlawful for a Jew to keep company
with men of other nations, God had showed him that
he was not to be bound any longer by such customs
or prejudices. Then he asks Cornelius what he
wants. Cornelius tells the story of his vision, and
then says to Peter, "Now therefore are we all here

present before God, to hear all things that are commanded thee of God." When a congregation and a minister meet on that footing, a minister like Peter, who comes, not to air out his own fancies, but to speak the things commanded him of God, and a congregation like Cornelius, ready and willing to hear what God will say, then we may expect the blessing of the Holy Spirit.

## II. The Sermon

Then Peter opened his mouth and spoke. He commenced with a declaration which has often and sadly been misinterpreted: "Of a truth I perceive that God is no respecter of persons: but in every nation he that feareth him, and worketh righteousness, is accepted with him." This has been strangely distorted to mean that if one lives a good decent life, is honest, charitable, even religiously inclined, he can get along without the gospel and without Christ. But this misses the point altogether. What Peter meant was that, through the agency of his dream, it had been brought home to him that the gospel of Christ was not intended for only those who are of the Jewish race, but was to be preached to men of every race and every speech; for their souls, too, were dear to God.

With that great introduction, Peter preached his memorable sermon. What do you think he said to this centurion? He might have eulogized him for his generosity and justice and purity of life; but if he had done so, I fancy I can see the countenance of the centurion fall; for with all his attainments in the path of virtue, there was in the centurion's heart a deep longing for peace and a happiness which thus far had eluded him. Or, if Peter had not known about the man's character, suppose he had reasoned with him of righteousness and temperance and exhorted him to be a kind, a just, and a religious, prayerful man? Then, too, I think I can see the centurion's countenance fall. All of this he had striven to be and yet he was not satisfied—not satisfied, either with the progress he had made, or with the blessedness that such progress had brought to him. But here was a preacher who did not disappoint his congregation. He preached Jesus to the centurion as Philip had preached Jesus to the Ethiopian. He told him of the life of Jesus, how he was full of the Holy Ghost, and went about doing good and healing all that were oppressed of the devil. Then he told him of his crucifixion, how they slew him and hanged him on a tree. But how on the third day, God raised him up and he appeared alive, not to the people generally but to witnesses who had known him before and who were qualified to testify of what they had seen and heard. Then he tells Cornelius, having thus given him the foundation facts of the gospel, what message this Jesus commanded his disciples to preach to the world. First, that to him all the prophets had witnessed. Christ was not an accident upon the field of time; but he came in the fullness of time and in fulfillment of God's great plan to redeem the world. Second, that Christ is ordained of God to be the judge of the quick and the dead, that before him who is both the world's Saviour and Judge, all men, the Jew and the Gentile, the Roman and the barbarian, the quick and the dead, the harlot and the saint, the thief and the devout centurion, must stand to give their account. And third, that through faith in his name men may receive the remission of their sins. This was the sermon which Peter preached to the centurion, and preached according to the commandment of the risen Jesus himself. If you want to know what Jesus desires his Church to say of him, read that last part of the tenth chapter of the Book of Acts. Would to God that all of us preachers could be as faithful to Christ's commandments as Peter was in this great sermon on this great occasion which marked the expansion of Christianity from a narrow sect to a world-conquering faith.

## III. The Results and the Implications of This Sermon

At the end of Peter's sermon, the Holy Ghost fell on all them that heard the Word. In this case the gift of the Holy Spirit was accompanied by that mysterious sign, the speaking with tongues. But we must not permit the obscurity of that gift to hide from us what the great work of the Holy Spirit here was—that is, repentance and faith in the Lord Jesus Christ. Such a sermon as Peter preached is the only kind of a sermon which can produce repentance and faith. It may not always do it, for the Spirit, like the wind, bloweth where it listeth. Nevertheless, it is the only kind of a sermon which can produce repentance and faith. It did so in this case. Cornelius gave such evidence of his faith and repentance that Peter himself proposes to him baptism, as the confirmation of his faith and his introduction into the Church of Jesus Christ. Peter did not stop by congratulating the centurion upon his faith and repentance, but told him to be baptized. Peter was not wiser than his Lord, who told his disciples to preach the gospel unto every creature, saying, "He that believeth and is baptized shall be saved." "If thou shalt confess with thy mouth the Lord Jesus, and shalt believe in thine heart that God hast raised him from the dead, thou shalt be saved. For with the heart man believeth unto righteousness; and with the mouth confession is made unto salvation."

The question is often asked, indeed it seems to have been asked from the very beginning, Does a moral man need a Redeemer? That question, it seems to me, was answered clearly and once for all in the conversion of this first man from the Gentile world. It is worth remembering that he was not a drunkard, or thief, or libertine; but the very pick of

the pagan world, just, devout, and charitable. When
Peter arrived in Caesarea I can imagine him asking
some man in the street where Cornelius lived, and
that man inquiring of Peter what his business might
be with Cornelius, and Peter responding, "I go to
preach the gospel to Cornelius; to tell him how
Christ died for sinners on the Cross, and through
faith in him men have the forgiveness of their sins."
But the man answers, "It must be some other Cornelius whom you are looking for. There is a noto-
rious brigand in the jail just now. Perhaps he is the
man. But certainly not the Roman centurion. Why,
you are only wasting your efforts in preaching to
him. The Gentiles honor him, the Jews respect him,
the soldiers adore him, widows and orphans rise up to
call him blessed, and I am told that he spends a good
part of every day in pious meditation and prayer.
Tell this Gospel of yours with its message of salvation
from sin to some of the drunken legionnaires who are
stationed here, or to some of the cruel publicans who
grind the face of the poor, or tell it to the harlots, the
men-stealers; tell it (let me whisper it) to our dis-
sipated Governor Felix and his paramour Drusilla,
but not to that good man Cornelius."

Yet, in all that pagan world, so sunken in de-
bauchery and sins unmentionable, it is to this devout
Roman soldier first of all, that the Holy Ghost directs
the apostle to preach the gospel of repentance and
salvation. If a man like Cornelius needed to repent

and be saved, then what shall we say for ourselves?
Yet the question will always be asked, although God
answered it so plainly in the conversion of Cornelius.
One says that he is a member of the lodge, and that
the principles which it inculcates seem to be much the
same as the principles of Christianity, indeed, are
based upon it. Or another describes a man who is
interested in every good work, who stands for the
highest things in the community, gives to every good
cause, and is a good husband and father in his home.
Is not this sufficient? Not if the conversion of Cornelius is a true fact and was inspired by the Holy
Ghost, because it tells us plainly that a man can be a
good citizen, an honest man, a charitable man, just
in his dealings, a good husband, or father, or son, and
yet lack the one great thing. If repentance and salvation were preached to a man like Cornelius, then
every man needs to repent and be saved.

Most of us will not have much difficulty in this
matter, because we can hardly claim the moral standing of Cornelius; and if a man like him had to repent,
and needed salvation through the shed blood of
Christ, then what of us? In the introduction to his
Confessions, Rousseau commences with these striking
words: "Such as I was I have declared myself to be,
sometimes vile and despicable; at others, virtuous,
generous, and sublime, even as thou hast read my
inmost soul. Power Eternal, assemble round thy
throne an innumerable throng of my fellow mortals.

Let them listen to my confessions, let them blush at my depravity, let them tremble at my sufferings, let each in his turn expose with equal sincerity the failings, the wanderings of his heart, and, if he dare, aver, 'I was better than that man.'" Who among my readers cares to accept that challenge?

Cornelius now passes from the New Testament stage. But in heaven he is glad to take his place in the company of redeemed souls, and, standing side by side with Mary of Magdala and the penitent thief, sing with them, his face, I think, not less radiant than theirs, the song of redemption, "Now unto him that hath loved us and hath washed us from our sins by his own blood."

# PETER AT THE GATE BEAUTIFUL

## XVIII

### Acts 3: 1-11

SOLOMON'S Temple was long gone, save for some fragments of it, such as Solomon's Porch; but the Temple of Herod had a glory of its own. Conspicuous among these splendors was the Corinthian Gate, and probably the Gate Beautiful of this beautiful story. It was made of Corinthian brass and covered with plates of silver and gold. It was fifty cubits high, and adorned after the most costly manner. It must have been of this gate and the Temple on that side of which Josephus writes in his *Jewish Wars*. At the rising of the sun it reflected back a fiery splendor and made those who forced themselves to look upon it to turn their eyes away, just as they would have done at the sun's rays. To strangers coming in from the distance, the Temple appeared like a mountain covered with snow. Such was the splendor of the Temple made with man's hands. In strange contrast was the Temple not made with hands—this poor lame beggar, who lay at the Gate Beautiful. The same contrast is

impressed upon the mind of the traveler who visits
the glorious cathedrals of Europe and is beset by
beggars on his way in and on his way out. This
man, now more than forty years old, had been lame
from his mother's womb. His birth brought joy into
his home, that Oriental joy which surpasses all
others. Every Jewish mother looked upon her child
as a potential Messiah. So this mother looked upon
her child. The weeks and the months went by; but
when the time came for her child to walk, this child
did not walk. Physicians and soothsayers and neighbors were consulted, and divers remedies were tried,
but all in vain. The child could not walk, and soon
it became apparent that he would never walk. There
was only one calling and future for such a child, and
that was to become a beggar. This for years had
been the profession of the lame man. Daily, neighbors or members of his family carried him up to the
Temple where he could beg. Temples are favorable
places for begging, for men coming in or out of the
Temple are supposed to be in moods of generosity
and worship. Here, then, at the Gate Beautiful of
the Temple, and his poor impotent body in strange
contrast with the glorious Temple of Herod, lay this
cripple and beggar.

Let us imagine his thoughts and reveries as he saw
the shadows playing on the face of the Gate Beautiful. Of what did he think? Perhaps of the blows
and curses he would receive if he came home empty-

handed. Perhaps, when he saw men walk by him in the full tide of vigor, he wondered why they could walk, but he could not. And this building, at the gate of which he lay, he said to himself, is God's Temple. But where is God? Does God see me? Does God care for a lame beggar?

But whatever his reveries, they were interrupted by the sound of footsteps. Peter and John were on their way up to the Temple. After the great events of the Ascension, and the Day of Pentecost, it would not have been strange if Peter and John had thought they could get along without the exercises of ordinary worship. But here they are at the ninth hour on their way up to the Temple to pray. There are some who are enthusiastic for special meetings, large convocations; but who cannot be counted on for the regular routine of Christian worship. Yet those who can be counted on, and who are found regularly at the appointed hours and in the appointed services of the Church, week after week, and year after year, are the ones upon whom the Church depends.

As they approached the spot where the beggar was lying, he thrust forth his hand, and with a professional wail asked alms of them. When the footsteps halted, the beggar's hope began to mount. Most of those whom he accosted passed by without a word. But these two men halted. They not only halted, but one of them, Peter, fastening his eyes upon him, said to him, "Look on us." That must have sent the hopes of the beggar still higher. Even those who gave to him rarely gave him a look. All that they did was to fling out a coin and pass by with averted gaze. But this time those whom he accosted not only stopped, but spoke to him, and said, "Look on us."

The beggar responded at once, expecting to receive something worth while. What must have been his disappointment, therefore, when Peter began, "Silver and gold have I none." This brought his hopes down to the ground again. Had he dared to say it, what he would have said would have been something like this: "Why did you stop if you had nothing to give me? Why did you tell me to look on you, if you had no alms for me? If you think this is a joke, it is a poor kind of a joke. Leave me to my memories and meditations, and go on to your hypocritical prayers in the Temple."

Thoughts like these, I suppose, were in his mind and words like these were almost on his tongue. But when Peter continued, "But such as I have give I thee," again the beggar's hopes began to rise. He means, thinks the beggar, that, although they have no silver or gold, they will give me what they have—coppers and pennies. That is what I usually receive, and it is better than nothing.

But it was something more than either silver or gold or copper that the beggar was to receive that

[ 200 ]

day. "Silver and gold have I none," said Peter; "but such as I have give I thee: In the name of Jesus Christ of Nazareth rise up and walk." Then Peter stretched out his right hand. There is the look of amazement and incredulity in the beggar's face. Perhaps he thought at first that Peter was not only mocking him as to silver and gold, but that now he was going to mock his lameness. What else could he mean by telling him, Rise up and walk? But Peter and John had told the man to look upon them. One look into the earnest countenance of Peter dispelled all doubt from the beggar's mind. Yes; he means it! I am to walk! With that, he seized the outstretched hand of the Apostle and was lifted to his feet. Immediately he felt the thrill of life and power in his feet and ankle bones; and the man who had not walked for more than forty years, walked and leaped and went into the Temple with Peter and John, praising God.

Christianity is a religion of giving. This is not strange, since it is founded upon the Unspeakable Gift of God's love. We miss it altogether when we make it a religion of seeking and of keeping. This is the first apostolic and Christian miracle, following immediately after the first Christian sermon. Peter gave the truth in the great sermon on the Day of Pentecost. Then he had a congregation of thousands; but he is just as earnest when his congregation is composed of one person, and that one person a

lame beggar. He gives this man what he has to give
—faith in the Name of Christ, and through that faith
the man is healed.

Peter had no silver or gold to give. Today the
greatest Church in the world bears his name. Thousands of Christians read his history as it is related
in the Gospels and in the Acts; and follow him in his
lofty expressions of faith and courage, his moments
of temptation and weakness and sin, his fall, his
restoration, and his apostolic ministry. Yet this
man, upon whom the eyes of the Christian world have
been fixed for ages, was one who said, "Silver and
gold have I none; but such as I have give I thee."

One might have the silver and gold in all the mints
of the land, and yet not be able to give the higher
and the abiding things. Moral character and influence are things which are more valuable than silver
and gold. Men with plenty of silver and gold may
not be able to give moral influence or character to
others. Had Peter and John been bad men, they
could not and would not have helped the lame man
that day. Peter said to the beggar, "Look on us."
Perhaps this was to get the beggar to concentrate his
thought and convince him of their earnestness. But
the phrase suggests also uprightness of life. They
could ask men, these apostles, to look on them. They
had nothing to hide, nothing of which they were
ashamed. He who lives in that way, so that he can
say to all men, "Look on us," makes a real contribu-

tion to the individual and to the community. He may not have much silver and gold, but he has something better to give. Ian Maclaren tells of how once, on a visit to the Highlands, he saw at the Communion on the Sabbath an old man, whom he had seen during the week breaking stone on the road, distributing the holy elements. When he asked his friends about it when he went home, how this could be, they told him that this old man, although he was a poor man, and had to break stones on the road for a living, knew more about God than any man in the village.

There will be those here today who will recall godly fathers and mothers. Yet you never think of them in the terms of money, whether they left you much or little, or nothing at all. If they left you the imprint of their character and their prayers, and the memory of their daily godly life, that is an inheritance incorruptible, undefiled, and that fadeth not away. The money which they left you may have disappeared long ago; but the influence of their godly example is an ever-present reality and power. Once, in a Virginia church, I saw an aged minister hold aloft a little black book and tell the congregation that all the money in the world could not purchase that book. It was not the book itself that was so valuable, for it was a cheap book, and its contents could be had in thousands of similar books throughout the world. What made it priceless to him was the fact that it was the Bible that his mother, now in heaven, had put in his trunk when he left home to go to college. Silver and gold she had none; but she had left him the memory of her faith and her prayers.

Sympathy and kindness are more valuable than silver and gold. Peter and John had nothing of the latter, but a great deal of the former. Had they not wished to help the poor lame man, had they not cared, they would not have stopped at the Gate Beautiful that day. The name of Christ would have had no power upon their lips. Sympathy is the distinguishing mark of the Christian man. Great spirits like Jesus are those who were moved with compassion. Ezekiel was called to his great prophecies after he himself had sat among the exiles in far-off Mesopotamia on the banks of the River Chebar. "I sat," he says, "where they sat." St. Paul cried out, "Who is weak, and I am not weak? Who is offended, and I burn not?" That was the reason that the golden-tongued preacher of Antioch, Chrysostom, in his great tribute to St. Paul called him "the heart of the world." There is an old tradition that before Moses was called by the Burning Bush in the Wilderness, God had seen him free a lamb which had been caught in the thicket. Marking his sympathy, he said, "Here is the man whom I will call to deliver my people. He has sympathy."

Faith cannot be bought and cannot be sold. When a man tried to buy it from Peter, Peter said, "Thy money perish with thee!" In one sense, no one can give another his faith. Yet we can help to increase the stock of mankind's faith. How poor and barren this world would be if all believers were taken out of it. Abraham was the greatest blessing because he was the greatest believer. When he came to die he did not own enough land for even a grave, and had to buy the cave of Machpelah from the sons of Heth. Yet when one stands on the floor of the Mosque at Hebron and looks down through the grating to where a dim light is burning near the ashes of Abraham, one thinks of how in him all nations of the earth have been blessed. Paul had no possessions, as the world counts them. His last will and testament mentions nothing but a few books and parchments and the old cloak which he had forgotten and left behind him in the house of Carpus at Troas. But who thinks of silver and gold when the name of Paul is mentioned?

In the sermon which he preached to the excited crowd which gathered to look with wonder on the healed man, Peter said that it was not he or John who had healed him; but that faith in the name of Christ had healed him. "His name through faith in his name hath made this man strong." The name of Christ, without faith in Christ, means no more in a religious sense than the name of Moses, or Caesar, or Napoleon, or Cromwell. It is only a name. But that name, with faith in the name, is still the greatest power in the world. It can cast out demons of hate and anger and envy and break the chains of the soul's bondage. Still it is the greatest power in the world. This is the victory that overcometh the world, even our faith. And what is faith? It is faith in the name of Christ.

Here are these first apostles working the first miracle after the first Christian sermon, and doing both in the name of Christ. Without that name, and faith in that name, the Christian is powerless and the Church has no witness. The disciple of Christ, if a true disciple, is the greatest ambassador and the most influential man in the world, because he alone can say to the world, "In the name of Jesus Christ of Nazareth, rise up and walk."

That is how these apostles lived. They lived and acted in the power of the name of Christ. Do we try to do that? Think of the things you cannot do in the name of Christ. When you hate or envy, you cannot do it in the name of Christ. When you revile or abuse another person, you cannot add to it those words, "In the name of Jesus Christ of Nazareth." When you take a mean or false advantage in business, you cannot write at the bottom of your agreement, "In the name of the Lord Jesus Christ." When you take up a reproach against your neighbor, you cannot do it in the name of Christ. When you utter what is false, or do what is unclean, you can never say, as you do it, "In the name of Jesus Christ of Nazareth." Thus the name of Christ is not only the only means of doing lasting good, but it is the chief means of defense against evil. Stop and ask yourself before you do or say or think certain things, "Can I do this, or say this, or think this, in the name of Jesus Christ of Nazareth?"

This lame man who was healed lay at the very Gate of the Temple. Think of that! It is possible to be, not only at the Gate of the Temple, or the Church, but actually inside the gate, and still be pitifully lame and weak. Yet the same power that healed the lame man as he lay there at the Gate Beautiful at the Temple, is able to heal the lame at the doors of our church, or in the pews of the church. How many different kinds of soul lameness there are! Are we not all conscious of a degree of paralysis and impotence which no physician or treatment of the world can cure? Only one thing can cure it, and that is faith in the name of Christ.

Again, then, this morning, the opportunity is passing by. Again the apostles are on their way to the Temple to pray. Again Peter says, "Silver and gold have I none, but such as I have give I thee." Once more Peter and John say, "Look on us." Again the representative of Christ and the Gospel stretches forth his hand and says unto you, "In the name of Jesus of Nazareth, rise up and walk." Who wants to walk? Who will take the outstretched hand? Look at that hand again. It is not the hand of a minister; it is not the hand of Peter, or the hand of John; it is a hand that is pierced with nails. It is the hand of Him who died upon the Cross, that through faith in His Name you might have forgiveness and Eternal Life. Will you take it?

# PETER AND THE ANGEL

## XIX

### *"And he smote Peter on the side"*
#### Acts 12: 7

HEROD, wretched syphilitic king, on his way to a terrible death himself, had put James, the brother of John, to death with the sword. We hear little of James in the Gospels, save that he was the brother of John. With John, James had asked through their mother, Salome, for a seat at the right hand of Christ in his glory. Jesus told them that such seats of honor and distinction in the Kingdom of God are not arbitrarily bestowed, but must be won by faithfulness and suffering. Then he asked them if they were ready to drink his cup and be baptized with his baptism. They both responded, "We are ready," little understanding, I suppose, what Jesus meant. Now James discovers what that cup is, and, first among the twelve disciples, he drinks Christ's cup of woe and wins the martyr's crown.

The killing of James pleased the populace in Jerusalem, whose minds were prejudiced against the disciples of Jesus; and when Herod saw that what he had done pleased the people, he stretched out his hand to kill Peter also. "He proceeded further." That is the natural history and sequence of all sin. Sin always turns out a second edition. One sin opens the way for, invites, suggests, sometimes demands, a second sin. Peter himself, about whom this story centers, had found that to be true in his own bitter experience. He denied his Lord once, and then, to protect himself, had to deny him again, and again, until the crowing of the cock and the look of Jesus brought him to himself.

The day had been set for Peter's execution. No reprieve is expected and no mercy from the cruel hand of Herod. Nevertheless, over at the house of Mary the mother of Mark, the church was having a prayer meeting. This was one of the most memorable prayer meetings in the history of the Church. Had we been there, we might have learned what a real prayer meeting is. Prayer without ceasing was made of the Church unto God. I wonder who did the praying. John, no doubt, was called upon first. He was the brother of the martyred James and the chief companion of Peter. If anyone's prayers could deliver Peter, John was the man. Then, perhaps Thomas, once the chief doubter, now a chief believer, led in prayer. And Nathanael and Philip; perhaps Mary herself uttered a prayer for Peter's release. They all believed in God and in the triumph of the Kingdom of His Son and their Saviour Jesus Christ; but, humanly speaking, they did not see how they could get along without Peter. He was their leader, their bold spokesman, and their great preacher. What would the Church do without him? And there he lay, bound in Herod's dungeon, guarded by sixteen soldiers, and when the sun rose on the morrow he was to be put to death. Never were there greater odds against prayer. On one side, Herod, the sixteen soldiers, the grim fortress walls of the dungeon, and the power of Rome itself; on the other side, a handful of men and women in a prayer meeting. How unequal the combat! And yet, as has often happened since, it was the prayer meeting that came out victorious.

Peter had quite a reputation by this time for breaking jail, having done it before. In order to guard against such a contingency, extraordinary precautions had been taken to prevent a jail delivery and the escape of Peter. He was bound in the innermost dungeon of the prison. Fourteen soldiers were stationed at the different doors and passageways between Peter's dungeon and the iron gate which opened upon the street. And there lay Peter, chained to a soldier on either side, sound asleep, while the church was praying for him. Peter, no doubt, had done his praying, too. He had committed his soul unto his Saviour, and therefore he could lie down and sleep. Once before we have seen

Peter asleep, and a guilty shameful sleep it was, for with James and John he had slept in the Garden of Gethsemane while his Lord was agonizing in prayer. But no blame attaches to this sleep. It is the sleep of the just, the sleep of complete submission to God's will. "So he giveth his beloved sleep."

Suddenly, at midnight, the dungeon chamber is flooded with brilliant light. When God commences the act, the darkness disappears before the light of his presence. An angel of the Lord smote him on the side, and said to him, "Arise up quickly." And his chains fell from his hands, yet so as not to awaken the soldiers to whom he had been chained. Who was this angel of the Lord? Perhaps the Angel of the Covenant, the Lord Jesus Christ himself. How beautiful a thing, if Christ himself had come down to answer that prayer of his faithful disciples in Mary's house and to deliver that Apostle who once had cursed him and denied him, but since then had so nobly fed the sheep of Christ.

Wherever you come upon Peter you cannot mistake him. He always acts frankly, impulsively, and here he is true to every portrait we have of him. It is clear that Peter was going to go out without his shoes, and without throwing around him his outer garment. But the angel—for angels are never in a hurry themselves—told him to put on his shoes and cast his garment about him. Peter did as he was told, and then followed the angel. So wonderful did it seem that he half thought it was only a dream that he was having; and yet the chains were no longer on his arms; and there lay the huge guards, to whom he had been fastened, sound asleep. He stepped over them, and came to the first door with its guards. Perhaps his heart was beating rapidly lest they should awaken and seize him; but he passed in safety to the second door with its guards, and thus came at length to the outer gate, the massive iron gate. Now he thought, "Who will open that gate? Better not to have been awakened at all than to have escaped thus far, get clear out to this iron gate only to find myself still a prisoner." But if that was Peter's feeling, it was quickly relieved; for as he came up to the iron gate it opened unto him of its own accord. That has always seemed to me a grand impressive verse in the Bible—that massive iron gate, opening of its own accord to let Peter out on to the street; a sort of symbol of God's complete mastery of all things in this world and how he is able to deliver out of the mouth of the lion. Once out on the street, Peter, still in sort of a daze, stamped his feet on the stones of the pavement and said to himself, "Now I know of a surety, that the Lord hath sent his angel, and hath delivered me out of the hand of Herod."

The deliverance of Peter by the angel is a beautiful and timeless parable of the way in which God

visits the souls of men, speaks to them, awakens
them, and gives them the opportunity of life and
salvation. There are times when, as it were, God's
angels come to smite us and invite us to follow them,
as surely as that angel did at that midnight hour
in the dungeon to Peter. These approaches of God
to our souls are the proof of man's importance and
worth. Not his great poetry, or his great archi-
tecture, or his great music, are the chief witnesses to
man's value and importance, but the fact that God
comes to visit him. "What is man, that thou art
mindful of him? and the son of man, that thou visit-
est him?" This will be the everlasting wonder, that
God does come to visit him in so many wonderful
and gracious ways. It is this fact which is the hope
and the thrill of preaching. Not that the preacher
can expect that anything he does or says, or any
approach of his to the heart and conscience of his
hearers, will accomplish anything; but that in the
providence of God, his message and his words may be
timed with and coincide with God's approach to the
soul. He may be speaking when the angel himself is
on the way.

Angels come and speak to us in the ordinary providences of life. I have often reflected upon this, that
the heavenly visitors who appear in the Old Testament come to men in the midst of the usual occupations of the day, as they came to Gideon on the
threshing floor, and to Abraham at his tent, and to

Manoah and his wife in the field. It requires no roll of thunder, no flash of flame, to let us know that God draws nigh to our soul. He has many secret doors by which he approaches men's lives.

Sometimes He comes by the door of sickness. Many times I have seen severe sickness and a near approach to the gates of death bring men, for a moment at least, to their true self. Then the soul is able to appraise at their true value the possessions of life. Then that which has been counted first has changed overnight into that which is last, and vice versa. Then hatreds die, and benevolence toward all men is awakened. Many a man lying so near to the other world that he has felt its cool breath upon his brow, has searched his heart and has resolved henceforth, should God spare his life, that it will be a life not without religion and faith, freed from habits of sin which have enthralled him and crippled him, and that the law of kindness will be the guide of his life. But too often, with returning health, the world returned also; this "present world," the worthlessness of which has been so clearly demonstrated, again deceives him and enslaves him.

Sometimes God enters one's life by the door of sorrow and affliction. Sorrow often floods the soul with the tides of penitence, and, as the angel troubled the pool at Siloam, so life's troubled waters have power to cleanse and purify the heart. I have seen many lives softened, humbled, and, for a time at least, completely changed by the visitation of sorrow; and I have marveled at the way in which grief can relax the grip of greed and selfishness and say to the dark spirits of envy, of hatred, and impurity, "Get thee behind me, Satan!" And seeing that, I have often said to myself, "If there were only some way in which men could be held up to the spirit that is now in them, and the views of life and its meaning which now dominate them could be kept from growing dim." But alas, with too many it is true that in a short time they are again their old worse, selfish, ungodly selves. The angel of sorrow smote them on the side. They started for a moment; were inclined to obey for a little; followed perhaps for a little distance; and then went back to their former ways. The grace of God they received in vain.

There is also what we might call the Angel of Conviction who comes to smite the soul in the midst of some iniquity or wrongdoing, or in a state of disobedience to God, and awakens it to repentance and to faith. This can happen not only through the ordinary means of grace, but, if God wills, in extraordinary ways. A striking illustration of how God can send an angel to smite with conviction and awaken from the sleep of sin and deliver a man from the chains of an evil bondage is the story of the conversion of Colonel Gardiner.

In a park near Prestonpans, not far from Edinburgh, there is a grave which bears the name of a

Colonel James Gardiner, who fell fighting gallantly when the royal army was defeated in the battle of Prestonpans by the Highlanders under Prince Charles Edward in 1745. His death is related in the pages of Scott's *Waverley* and the remarkable story of his conversion and visitation is told by Philip Doddridge, the author of many of our hymns, who was his friend and preached his funeral sermon.

The son of an officer, he had followed his father in the profession of arms, and through gallantry in action and personal attractiveness soon rose to be a Colonel. On the field of battle he had many narrow escapes from death, but none of these encounters with death sobered his mind or won him from the licentious living to which he had abandoned himself. The prayers of his widowed and devout mother were apparently to go unanswered. On a July Sabbath evening in 1719 he had been dining with a company of dissolute companions. The company broke up at 11 o'clock. At midnight he had an assignation with a married woman. As he sat in his chambers, impatiently waiting for the clock to strike the hour, he took out of his portmanteau a book which his mother had put in it when he left home. It was *The Christian Soldier, or, Heaven Taken by Storm*, a strange prophecy of what was shortly to happen. As he was glancing through its pages, not heeding what he read, a sudden blaze of light seemed to fall on the page. He glanced up, supposing that some

accident had befallen the candle. As he lifted his
eyes he saw a visible representation of Christ on
the Cross, surrounded with glory. Then there came
what seemed to be a voice, which said, "Oh, sinner,
did I suffer this for thee, and are these the returns?"
It is possible, as Doddridge intimates, that it was
a dream. But dream or not, it makes no difference
as to the moral and spiritual result. At once he knew
himself to be the vilest sinner who all his lifetime
had been crucifying Christ anew by his sins. He
was sure that the justice of God required that such
an enormous sinner should be made an example of
everlasting vengeance. Yet his keenest pangs were
not from any dread of hell, but from the sense of
having been so ungrateful a monster to Him whom he
now saw pierced for his transgressions.

Convinced of his doom, Gardiner nevertheless determined that the remainder of his life should be
God-fearing and decent, and he cast himself upon
the mercy of God. For months no relief came to
him; but at once the corrupt fires of his nature sank
and went out, leaving him with an abhorrence for
the licentious sensualities to which he had been a
slave all his life, and to which he had been so devoted that he had said that Omnipotence itself could
not reform him without destroying his body and
giving him another. But now the chains of his dis-
gusting bondage fell from him. In the course of
time the terrors of the law were supplanted by the

assurance of peace and forgiveness, and the remaining years of his life were a noble and courageous witness to the Christ who had sought him and found him. As he lay dying on the fatal field of Prestonpans, he said to a Highland officer whom he saw lying near him, also fatally wounded, "You are fighting for an earthly crown; I am about to receive an heavenly."

There is but one explanation of such a change, and that is Jesus Christ. He who cast the legion of devils out of the Gadarene still casts out evil spirits from human hearts. When the angel smote Gardiner on the side, he arose and followed Him.

When God comes to smite the soul and awaken it, everything depends upon what the awakened man does, for there are two sides to conversion. There is God's side, and man's side. Conviction is God's part; faith and obedience are man's part. Suppose that when Peter was smitten that night on the side by the angel, he had just rolled over between those two soldiers and said to himself, as he was tempted to do, "This is only a dream." Or suppose he had roused himself to a sitting posture and then sunk down in sleep again? Or suppose, when he was awakened and was told to follow the angel, he had said to himself and to his angel, "It's no use. There are sixteen soldiers and an iron gate between me and the open air. There's no use trying to escape. Even an angel has not strength enough to get me out of this dungeon." If Peter had followed any of those courses, he never would have been delivered, and on the morrow his head would have fallen under the bloody sword of Herod. But instead of that, Peter arose at once, did everything that the angel told him to do, followed where the angel led, and so marched to his freedom and deliverance.

It is dangerous to hesitate or doubt when God speaks to us and touches our conscience. In worldly matters, in the impulses which come to us from our lower nature, it is always wise to pause and hesitate, to take these impulses home with us and sleep over them; but not so with these God-born impulses to which none of us is a stranger, and which are sent of God for our deliverance as truly as the angel came to visit and deliver Peter. Even if we could count on these visitations and impulses being repeated, we cannot count upon our reaction to them. When the angel strikes, when God draws nigh to you, when you know that you are hearing something more than your own voice, than the voice of this world, arise and follow, not then, but now; not tomorrow, but today, for that way lie liberty, hope, and Life Eternal.

# PETER AT THE IRON GATE

## XX

### *"They came unto the iron gate"*

Acts 12: 10

SOME of you have come to that gate. All of us will one day stand before it. Written on the gate are names like these: Sorrow, Pain, Sin, Remorse, Fear, Death.

Herod, the wicked and diseased king, thinks that he can dam up the stream of Christian faith flowing out of Jerusalem by murdering the apostles. First he killed James the brother of John. What resources God must have who can afford to let James die, for James was one of the Sons of Thunder, specially honored by Jesus who took him into the presence of death, up to the Mount of Transfiguration, and to the place of his agony in Gethsemane. Yet God lets Herod take him and kill him. "James the brother of John he slew with the sword." James had once said that he was able to drink the cup of Christ and be baptized with his baptism. Now he knows what that means. God let Herod kill him because

He has more use for James' head on the block than in a pulpit.

But with Peter it was to be different. Having killed James, Herod stretched forth his hand to kill Peter also. It was to be a Passover spectacle. Because of his past record for breaking jail, Herod takes unusual precautions with Peter, placing him in the inner dungeon of the prison and guarding him with sixteen Roman soldiers. But by all the Christians of Jerusalem prayer was made unceasingly for Peter's release. Had they not prayed as earnestly for James' release? I have no doubt they had. But their prayer had not been answered. Yet they are not discouraged. A vast combination had been effected to see that Peter's head came off after the feast. He was bound with two chains forged by the best smith in Jerusalem to the soldiers who lay on either side of him. Sixteen soldiers in all were charged to keep Peter, and if he escaped their lives would be forfeited. These men had as much regard for Peter's life as they had for one of the insects which crawled over the prison walls. Within the prison there were two wards, each with a wall and a gate, and around the prison was the outside wall with its iron gate. Over all the prison was the jailor and after him was Herod, the king, and his guard of soldiers; and far away, the Roman emperor—all banded together to kill Peter. On the other side there was nothing but a prayer meeting in the house of Mary, the mother of John Mark. Here were a few humble men and women on their knees. The combat appears to be unequal; yet it is the prayer meeting which will be victorious.

Meanwhile, Peter was sleeping. I suppose he was the only Christian sleeping that night in Jerusalem. The two soldiers to whom he was bound were also sleeping. Perhaps they were dreaming of some rough encounter with the barbarians on the banks of the Danube or the Rhine. Between them lies Peter sound asleep. This time it is not the guilty slumber of Gethsemane, but the peaceful sleep of faith. Let us leave for a moment this chamber where Peter is sleeping and cross the street to Herod's palace. Here, instead of cold, damp flags, is a soft silken couch with scented coverings; and here two soldiers attend the sleeper's couch, just as they did Peter's; only in the case of Peter they are there to keep his friends from delivering him; whereas, in the case of Herod they are there to keep his enemies from killing him. Yet, strange though it seems, it is the man with hard chains on his hands and ankles, and lying on the bare floor, who sleeps; whereas the man on the silken couch cannot sleep. Guilt awakes and cannot, be put to sleep; whereas faith sleeps like a child on its mother's breast, or like Jesus on the cushion in the storm on Galilee.

A few more hours and it will all be over. The mob will shout, the headsman's sword will flash, and Peter will have gone to join James and receive the martyr's crown. But at the last moment God acts. God might have acted before; but he waits until the last hour. Now for darkness, there is light; in place of silence, a voice; in place of slumber, action. Suddenly, the prison was filled with light. The angel smote Peter on the side and said, "Rise up quickly." As he did so his chains fell from him. It took an angel to break his chains, but Peter was able to throw his own mantle about his shoulders and put on his sandals, and this the angel told him to do. Then they started on their way out of the prison. At the gate of the first ward they stepped over the two sleeping soldiers, and as they did so one of them stirred uneasily and Peter's heart almost stopped. Down the corridor they went until they came to the gate of the second ward, where more soldiers lay sleeping. Here Peter's sandal brushed the thigh of one of the soldiers, and seizing his sword he raised himself from the floor with an oath; but in a moment fell back and was sound asleep. Down the last corridor Peter followed his angel to the gate that opened to the city. This was the last barrier, the massive iron gate. When he saw that gate, perhaps Peter's hopes fell. I wonder if he said to himself, "It would have been better not to have been roused out of sleep at all, than to get this far and then have my hopes dashed." But lo, as they came up to the iron gate, it opened unto them of its own accord. No key was thrust into the lock; there was no noise of drawn bolts; but silently, majestically, slowly, the massive gate swung open, and Peter stepped out on the street a free man. When he realized that he was actually free, and that it was not all a dream, he started at once for the home of Mary, and when he had been admitted the prayer meeting was turned into a thanksgiving service.

The Iron Gate! Have you ever been there? You wet it with your tears, or beat on it with your hands. It was impossible to go forward; experience could suggest no plan; counsel could give no help; hope flashed no light; and even prayer seemed to be thrust back in mockery by this grim barrier. As men go through life they will sometimes find themselves at the iron gate. The gate blocks further progress. And yet, like this iron gate which let Peter out, the gate of their difficulty suddenly opened unto them. The cloud lifted; the burden rolled from their back; the storm was over, the path was straight before them. God has done that for many a man in the past, and He is still able to do it for His people, for His arm is not shortened that it cannot save, nor His ear dull that He cannot hear.

## I. THE IRON GATE OF PERSONAL PERPLEXITY AND DIFFICULTY

There are many people today who are standing before an iron gate of economic circumstance. There has been a sudden change in their fortune, dividends cut off, employment lost, and they are faced with the necessity of earning their living in some new way. Many of them have no equipment, no experience, no skill, nothing that has a market value. It is like facing a stone wall. Yet the iron gate has opened before and can open again. Or another has trained carefully for some work or profession and no door of opportunity has opened, no connection could be established, the heart was sad and hope sank. Then one day the iron gate suddenly opened. Those who stand before such an iron gate today ought not to despair, but have hope and courage. The way will be made clear, and you will find your place and your work in the world.

Again, the iron gate may be a home or a family problem or difficulty. Home has ceased to be a refuge and has become a problem. It may be one personal relationship, or personal health, a thorn in the flesh in your own, or, what is worse, in another's flesh; or it may be some problem of life outside the family relationship. Labor, thought, patience, tears, entreaties, remonstrance, prayers, all have failed to solve the problem or lift the blockade. Then perhaps, when all hope or expectation of a change has died out of your heart, the difficulty adjusts itself, the burden rolls from your shoulder, and the iron gate opens unto you, apparently, of its own accord.

## II. The Iron Gate of Sorrow and Affliction

How many thousands tonight are standing before that gate. I meet with them and speak with them almost every day. There they stand, anointing the gate with ineffectual tears. Here is one who was going on prosperously in his course. Troops of friends were about him, loved companions made life what it was. Then, suddenly, without warning, he found himself alone, facing an iron gate of silence and sorrow. Midday had changed into midnight, spring into winter, and music into silence. Duty, ambition, desire, love—all have ceased to stir or animate the breast. The driving power of life is gone and life's urge has departed. All that the man can do is to try in vain and uselessly implore. O iron gate of sorrow! How many thousands this morning stand mute and helpless and heartless before thy grim, unanswering portal!

But for the comfort and hope of all who stand before that iron gate of sorrow, let it be said that that is not the whole history. Others have stood there before you, and the future seemed as blank and dark to them as it does now to you. Time, reflection, friendship, religion, and the blessed and inescapable duties of the day did their silent and unobtrusive ministry. Life went on, and they went on. Their grief remained, but not the bitterness of it. The memory of their sorrow is still with them, but it is sacred and purifying. A deeper meaning came into their life; and now they can use their own experience to comfort and strengthen others who stand before that same grim gate.

### III. Death Itself, to Our View, Is an Iron Gate

As we go down the third ward toward this gate the prospect is not reassuring.

> "E'en such is time, who takes in trust
>    Our youth, our years, and all we have,
> And pays us but in age and dust;
>    Who in the dark and silent grave,
> When we have traveled all our ways,
> Shuts up the story of our days." [1]

Yes, certainly death's gate looks like a thus-far-and-no-farther. Science, philosophy, fancy, and superstition have all tried in vain to pick the lock of this cruel and massive gate. Men have talked airily of death and all its ways, have walked merrily down toward it as if no iron gate were there. Yet we know it is there: we cannot blind our eyes to it; and the nearer we get to it, the more ironlike it looks. Yet God can open that gate as He opened the gate of Peter's dungeon that midnight in Jerusalem. This gate in Peter's dungeon opened, the

---

[1] Sir Walter Raleigh (found in his Bible).

record says, "into the city." That is always true of a gate. It shuts in, but it also lets out. To the Christian believer death is an iron gate that opens into the City which hath foundations, whose builder and maker is God. If the Christian and believing dead could speak to us, and tell us of that City, how strange to us now would seem our fears, our tears, our misgivings, and our dismay, as we stand before the iron gate of death.

"Could we but climb where Moses stood,
    And view the landscape o'er,
Not Jordan's stream, nor death's cold blood,
    Should fright us from the shore." [2]

## IV. The Iron Gate of Sin

This is the darkest and heaviest gate of all. Suddenly, it has come down across our way, grim, dark, insurmountable. Sin casts men into prison, commits them unto sixteen soldiers of remorse, and then shuts them in with this grim and massive gate of retribution. Who knows who here today is standing before that gate of sin? No wish, no fancy, can remove the fact that there has been transgression, that the soul has suffered, and that the wages of sin is death. The gate is there, and you cannot pass through it. You cannot go around it or climb over it. What you have written, you have written. Yet

[2] Isaac Watts.

this is a gate which the mercy of God can open. He has opened it before for thousands upon thousands of those who have confessed their sin and have sought His mercy in Christ. The pierced hand of Jesus puts the key of His forgiveness into the lock of the gate of sin and the prisoner goes free. The gate opens unto him into the city of peace and forgiveness.

Traveling in Norway, as the ship sails slowly through the beautiful and silent fjords, with the grand mountains rising all about you, and beautiful cascades making sweet music as they hurry down the perpendicular cliffs on their way back to their mother, the sea, the passenger on the deck of the vessel will see the channel in front narrowing until it looks like a blind end. You seem to be sailing straight into the mountain. A few hundred yards further, and you are sure the prow of the steamer will strike on the iron cliffs. But just when progress seems impossible, the channel opens up and the steamer glides out upon another fjord of entrancing beauty. So it is with the iron gates up to which we come on the pilgrimage of life, whether it be the iron gate of present and personal difficulty, or temptation, or sorrow, or sin, or death itself. In God's own way and in God's own time the gate will swing open and we shall pass out into the city.

This gate opened of itself; and yet not of itself. True, neither Peter nor the angel pushed it open;

but other hands, though invisible, were pushing on it. I mean the hands of all those who that night in the home of Mary were unceasing in their prayer on behalf of Peter. All of them, even the youngest and the humblest, had a part in opening the iron gate for Peter. That lets us know the power of intercession. Remember in your prayers all those who may be standing today at their iron gate. For yourself, have patience and be in prayer. Every gate which shuts in, is also a gate which will let you out. Thus the Iron Gate becomes a Gate of Gold, on which are written the characters of Divine Love and Mercy.

# PETER'S FIFTEEN DAYS WITH PAUL

## XXI

*"After three years I went up to Jerusalem
to see Peter and abode with him
fifteen days"*

Galatians 1: 18

WONDERFUL fifteen days! What would we not give now for an account by either Peter or Paul of that memorable visit. But what was spoken by them, or thought by them, must be left to our imagination.

Peter and Paul are the two towering personalities of the Christian Church. James the brother of our Lord was a man of great influence and leadership in the early Church at Jerusalem. After the work of Peter and Paul had been done, the Apostle John, the man of eagle wings and lofty contemplation, did his work and made his great contribution to the literature of the New Testament. But Peter and Paul stand out as the chief pillars of the Church. In a real sense, after our Lord himself, they are the founders of the Christian Church. Very early in

Christian history we find their names linked together. Churches and cathedrals today bear the names of both apostles, and frequently we see their statues standing side by side: Peter always with the keys, the symbol of his authority; and Paul always with the sword, the gladiator of the Word of God and the Gospel.

So far as we know, Peter and Paul met one another just three times in their life. The first time was at Jerusalem, three years after Paul's conversion, when he went up to Jerusalem and spent two weeks with Peter. The second time was fourteen years after this first visit, and again at Jerusalem, when Paul went up to Jerusalem with Barnabas and Titus to defend the right of the Gentiles to come into the Church without circumcision. There Paul met James and Peter and John, whom he speaks of as the "pillars of the Church," and who accepted his proposition that the Gentiles need not subscribe to the particularities of the Mosaic Law. Peter was a pleader for the rights of the Gentiles at this memorable conference, and reminded those who were in attendance that it was he who had been chosen of God to give the gospel to the Gentiles first of all, meaning his preaching of the gospel to Cornelius and his household. Having won, with Peter's help, the great battle for Christian liberty, Paul continued his work among the Gentiles, it being the understanding that Peter's work was to be among the Jews chiefly, and

Paul's among the Gentiles. "For he that wrought effectually in Peter to the apostleship of the circumcision, the same was mighty in me toward the Gentiles." (Gal. 2: 8.)

The next and, perhaps, the last meeting between the two apostles, was at Antioch, where the work among the Gentiles had its beginning, and whence the first missionaries went forth into the heathen world. Peter was at Antioch on a visit, and mingled freely with the Gentile Christians and ate with them. But when "certain from James," who was the leader among the Jewish Christians at Jerusalem, came down to Antioch, Peter, fearing that they would be offended at his association with the Gentile Christians, separated himself and ceased to meet with them and to eat with them. Other of the Jewish Christians followed his example. Even Barnabas, the close friend of Paul, ceased to associate with the Gentile Christians.

This inconsistent and cowardly conduct on the part of Peter aroused the righteous indignation of St. Paul, who never showed to a better advantage. Rising in a convocation of the Christians at Antioch, he openly accused Peter of inconsistency and rebuked him to his face. He pointed out that it was outrageous, that Peter should feel that as a Jewish Christian he could live as a Gentile and yet at the same time compel the Gentile Christians to live as Jews. It had more serious implications, too; for if these Jewish rites were necessary for Gentile Christians, then the death of Christ was unnecessary, and men would be justified, not by faith in Christ, but by works of the law.

We can imagine what a scene that must have been —St. Paul, the younger man, and a bitter persecutor of the Church before his conversion, rebuking the great Peter. It was a courageous act, and the Church today owes a debt of gratitude to St. Paul. That there was no final breach between the apostles we can gather from the fact that Paul in an argument on Christian freedom of conscience, in his First Letter to the Corinthians, makes an incidental reference to the fact that Peter led about a wife with him, and thus recognizes Peter as a worthy missionary and preacher of the gospel. What Peter's thought about Paul was, we gather from the close of his Second Letter, where he speaks of Paul as "our beloved brother," and refers to Paul's Epistles, apparently, as of equal authority with the Old Testament Scriptures. He also says, incidentally, that in these Epistles of Paul there are some things hard to be understood. We all agree with Peter as to that. But Paul might have returned the compliment and said that there were some things in the Epistles of Peter also which are hard to understand and which the unlearned and unstable wrest as they do the other Scriptures. Among these difficult things is Peter's statement that Christ went and preached unto the spirits in prison.

Few passages in the Scriptures have aroused greater curiosity or occasioned more dispute than that.

We know that Paul was in Rome. We have no conclusive evidence from the New Testament that Peter was ever there. Certainly it is unlikely that he was there before or during Paul's first imprisonment at Rome. It is inconceivable that Paul should have left out the name of Peter in the long list of his greetings to the Christians at Rome in the last chapter of Romans, if Peter was in Rome at that time. It would be strange also that Paul should not have mentioned in any of the Epistles written at Rome the presence of Peter, if Peter was there at that time. The one New Testament statement which may mean that Peter was at Rome is in the greeting which Peter sends at the close of his First Epistle: "The Church that is at Babylon, elected together with you, saluteth you; and so doth Marcus my son." If by Babylon is meant Rome, as the name undoubtedly implies in the Apocalypse, then this means that Peter was at Rome. Outside of the New Testament there is a fairly strong Christian tradition that Peter went to Rome and suffered martyrdom about the same time as St. Paul. The supposed bodies of the two apostles were moved to the Catacombs in the year 258 to save them from desecration by the pagans. The body of St. Peter is supposed to repose today under the great dome of St. Peter's and

the body of St. Paul under the noble church of St.
Paul's without the Walls.

Let us try to imagine something of what transpired at that first of the three meetings between the
apostles when Paul was for fifteen days the guest
of Peter. In doing this, let us remember that in
the most explicit language St. Paul declares that the
gospel which he preached he received by a revelation and not by man, and that none of the leaders of
the church at Jerusalem added anything to him—
that is, that they imparted to him nothing of importance so far as his gospel that he preached was
concerned. At the same time, it is quite conceivable,
indeed probable, almost certain, that the general
history of Christ's ministry in the flesh and many
of the great events of his passion and resurrection
could have been communicated to St. Paul by Peter.

*Peter:* "Paul, I am glad indeed to see thee. Barnabas has spoken to me of thee. Many of our
brethren here, I know, have feared to greet thee and
to accept thee as a true disciple of Christ, and now a
proclaimer of the gospel."

*Paul:* "Nor is that strange, Peter, since they know
that I imprisoned and beat in every synagogue them
that believed on Jesus; and when the blood of the
martyr Stephen was shed, I also was standing by and
consenting unto his death, and kept the raiment of
them that slew him."

*Peter:* "Yes, that is true; but I am glad to greet

thee as a true brother in Christ, and by thy miraculous conversion a pattern to them who shall hereafter believe on Christ to life everlasting."

*Paul:* "To me there hath been revealed the fullness of the gospel of redemption, that Jesus was the Messiah, that to him all the prophets bear witness, that his death on the Cross provides an atonement for sin, that through faith in him men have the forgiveness of sin and the gift of the Holy Spirit; and that he shall come again in the clouds with great glory, and that with him we shall dwell in everlasting peace."

*Peter:* "Yes; thou hast received the truth, St. Paul. I can add nothing to it."

*Paul:* "But, Peter, I would hear from thine own lips something of those years that thou didst walk by the side of the Messiah."

*Peter:* "The sun is sinking and the heat of the day is past. Let us go yonder to the Mount of Olives, there where often His disciples were wont to sit with him and listen to the words of wisdom from his mouth. We can sit there together while I discourse with thee of the great days that are past, and also of the great days that are to come."

(They ascend to the Mount of Olives.)

*Peter:* "Here from this Mount we can see the whole country, and the whole history, as it were, of the days of His flesh. Yonder, Paul, in that far-off valley thou canst see the River Jordan. It was there first of all that my brother Andrew brought me to Jesus. There it was that, looking upon me, He said, 'Thou art Peter, and upon this rock I will build my Church.' And yonder, Paul, far in the distance is the Sea of Galilee, and on the northern shore of that sea, Capernaum, where I dwelt. It was on that sea that, after a miraculous draught of fishes, I fell at his feet and besought him to depart from me, a sinful man, and there, too, it was that, fishing one day with Andrew and our partners, James and John, I heard him call us to him and say, 'Follow Me, and I will make you fishers of men.' All that country of Galilee, Paul, is sacred ground to me, for in almost every village I have some memory of our Lord. Away yonder to the north of the Sea of Galilee is the desert place where Jesus took us apart one day and said, 'Whom do men say that I am?' There it was given me of the Spirit to answer, 'Thou art the Christ, the Son of the living God.' That sea, too, recalls my boasting and my weakness; the night when, in the midst of the storm at the fourth watch, he came walking to us on the sea, and I asked him to let me walk to him on the sea. For a time all went well, but when I looked away from him and saw the waves, my courage failed and I began to sink; but when I cried, 'Save, Lord, or I perish!' he took me by the hand and brought me into the boat. And yonder, away to the northwest, is the peak of Tabor. There he was transfigured before John and James and me; and I, overcome with the glory of it, and thrilled with the thought of Moses and Elijah, cried out, 'It is good for us to be here. Let us build here three tabernacles; one for thee, and one for Moses, and one for Elijah.' But here below us, and all about us, too, are memories both sad and glorious. Yonder, near the wall of the city, is the house where we met to eat the Passover. There it was that he washed our feet and wiped them with towels. There, too, it was that when he was sad and heavy-hearted, and had said that one of us should betray him, I boasted that, though all should forsake him and flee, I would be faithful to the end. What follows, Paul, is too painful for me to relate, and will be too painful for thee to hear. Silence is best."

*Paul:* "Tell all, Peter, and hide nothing. Remember that I, too, have painful memories. Remember that I was a blasphemer and a persecutor of Christ and his Church. If thou hast bitter memories, so have I, for there it was, Peter, on that rocky hillside, just off the gate at the northwest wall of the city, that I held the garments of those who stoned the martyr Stephen. We both have bitter memories; yet amazing grace hath found us and saved us."

*Peter:* "Then, Paul, I will tell thee all and hide nothing. When we came out of the city on that night and crossed the Kedron, we entered into the Garden of Gethsemane which lies there just beneath us. The eight disciples he left not far from the gate, but John, James, and myself he took with him into the midst of the Garden. Then, asking us to watch with him, he went off a stone's throw and began to pray. We watched for a little, but our hearts were heavy and soon we were fast asleep. Twice he came and awakened us, saying, 'Could ye not watch with me one hour?' But when he came the third time and awakened us, he said, 'Sleep on now, and take your rest: behold, the Son of man is betrayed into the hands of sinners.' When the Scribes and the Pharisees and the mob led by Judas came to take him, and I saw a servant of the High Priest strike Him, I could not contain myself, and drawing my sword I smote off the ear of the servant of the High Priest. Never to my dying hour, Paul, can I forget the tenderness with which Christ healed the ear of the man I had wounded. When they led Him away, most of the disciples fled. John and I, however, followed afar off. Yonder, Paul, where that high roof is, is the palace of the High Priest Caiaphas. There it was that, sitting by the fireside, I thrice denied my Lord. When I was cursing and denying for the third time, they led him out from the priest's chambers, and hearing my cruel oaths he turned and looked upon me. What a look, Paul, that was! Thou canst not imagine the sweetness and the grace of it."

*Paul:* "Yes, Peter, I can well imagine. Remember, Peter, you are talking to the chief of sinners. That same Jesus looked upon me, full of blasphemy and breathing out threatenings and slaughters, at the Gate of Damascus and said, 'Saul, Saul, why persecutest thou me?'"

*Peter:* "And that, Paul, was what that look said to me on that awful night, 'Peter, Peter, why persecutest thou me?' Just then the cock crew, and when I thought thereon, I went out into the night and wept bitterly."

*Paul:* "I, too, Peter, know the blackness of that night. For three days I sat in darkness and in bitterness in the house of Judas at Damascus, full of sorrow and shame that I had persecuted Jesus."

*Peter:* "But in that bitter night, Paul, I remembered what he had said to me at the supper, 'I have prayed for thee, that thy faith fail not.' Terrible as my shame and agony were, I remembered his prayer for me and had hope. I repented and was saved."

*Paul:* "Then thou wast with Him at the Cross?"

*Peter:* "No; I did not see Him die upon the Cross. All that dreadful day and the next day I lay in misery at the home of John. On the morning of the third day, the women came and told us that the sepulcher was empty. John and I ran to the sepulcher. John, who is younger, outran me; but when I reached the sepulcher, I found John standing at the entrance, afraid to go in. But when I saw that the sepulcher was empty, I went in and saw the grave-clothes lying. And then entered in John also, and believed."

*Paul:* "But thou didst not see him?"

*Peter:* "Not then! but at the third hour, when I was wandering disconsolate there in the Garden of Gethsemane, suddenly He appeared unto me. It was the same Lord, and yet a new glory and majesty seemed to be about Him. But it was the same tender voice that spake. He told me that I was forgiven, and that I was to feed his sheep. And yonder, Paul, by the Sea of Galilee, He appeared again unto me. This time with John and five others of the Apostles. There He said openly before the others what He had said to me alone by that tree in the Garden of Gethsemane, 'Feed my sheep.'"

*Paul:* "Thou wast a fisherman, Peter, and I was bred and trained in the school of Gamaliel. Yet, after all, our experience has been much the same. We both were great sinners. Thou, Peter, didst deny him with an oath; but I persecuted Him, cursed Him, and made others curse Him. After His Resurrection, He appeared unto thee by thyself, Peter, and first of all the apostles, and forgavest thee thy sin. To me also, full of murder and hatred, he appeared as unto one born out of due time, and sent me forth to preach his love to the Gentiles. Thou wast sent to feed the sheep, Peter, the lost sheep of the house of Israel; and I to find the lost sheep among the Gentiles."

(The year 63. Peter and Paul in the Mamertine Dungeon at Rome, awaiting execution.)

*Paul:* "Many years have passed, Peter, since last we met at Antioch. Thou hast no hard feeling, Peter, for the rebuke I gave thee there?"

*Peter:* "No, Paul, faithful are the wounds of a friend. Thou spakest only the truth. But tell me, Paul, of thy last journeys. I knew that thou hadst appealed unto Caesar, and that thou wast taken to Rome and preached the gospel in thine own hired house, and that thou didst win for Christ saints out of Caesar's household. Where, then, Paul, didst thou go?"

*Paul:* "To Spain, Peter, then back to Macedonia. Then down to Crete, where I left Titus; thence to Asia again; and thence into Macedonia. There at Nicopolis, where I was wintering, I heard of the persecution of the saints in Rome and came hither to cheer them and to share their fate. Now, Peter, how camest thou here?"

*Peter:* "I came to Rome whilst thou wast absent. With me were thy two old friends and companions, Silas and Mark."

*Paul:* "Well do I remember them. Mark was with me on the first great journey of the gospel, when we sailed from Antioch for Cyprus. In Asia Minor Mark turned back. On the next journey we parted; he went with Barnabas, Silas with me. But

I rejoice to know that he has been faithful to the Lord and unto thee."

*Peter:* "When the persecutions of Nero broke out, I bade Mark and Silas flee the city. They are now on their way to Corinth. The disciples of our Lord came to me and urged me also to flee the anger of the Beast. The Lord touched the heart of the jailor and he set me free. I left the city and had gone some distance along the Appian Way when I met our Lord."

*Paul:* "And what saidst thou to him, Peter?"

*Peter:* "I said to him, 'Whither goest thou, Lord?' He answered, 'I go to Rome to be crucified again.' That word smote my heart. I turned back to the city again, was arrested at the gate and thrust once more into this prison."

*Paul:* "Tomorrow, then, Peter, we shall both die."

*Peter:* "Yes, we shall receive the crown of glory that the Chief Shepherd shall give us. Long have I waited for this end. When I met the Lord by the Sea of Galilee after his Resurrection, and he said to me, 'Feed my sheep,' he then added, 'Verily, verily, I say unto thee, When thou wast young, thou girdedst thyself, and walkedst whither thou wouldest: but when thou shalt be old, thou shalt stretch forth thy hands, and another shall gird thee, and carry thee whither thou wouldest not.' Tomorrow, then, I shall be stretched upon a cross. If the executioner grants it, I shall be crucified head downward, for I am not worthy to die on the cross as my Lord died for me. Thou, Paul, being a citizen of Rome, wilt be put to death by the sword."

*Paul:* "Thou, Peter, on the cross; I by the sword. Yet for both of us, Peter, it will be far better. We shall be with the Lord. Heaven is as near by the sword as by the cross."

*Peter:* "Yes, we shall receive the inheritance incorruptible, undefiled, and that fadeth not away."

*Paul:* "This mortal shall put on immortality. This corruption shall put on incorruption."

*Peter:* "Through yonder window, Paul, steals the light of the day—our last day upon earth. Soon will come the executioner."

*Paul:* "Yes; Peter, the last day of earth is dawning. Yet it is also the first day of heaven. The everlasting day has come."

*Peter:* "Pray for me, Paul. I feel strong and confident now; but I remember how once before when I thought I was brave, I fell. When I think of the cross, the nails, the hammers, the rending of the flesh, the—"

*Paul:* "Be of good courage, Peter. The Lord will stand by us unto the end."

*Peter:* "The executioner! he has come!"

*Paul:* "Farewell, Peter, we shall meet before the Throne of the Lamb. Now let us greet one another with an holy kiss. The Grace of the Lord Jesus Christ, and the Love of God, and the Communion of the Holy Spirit be with thee."

*Peter:* "Peace be with thee, Paul. And with me! It is morning! The Day! Eternal Day has come! The Daystar hath risen in our hearts."